N. KARAZIN

CRANES
FLYING
SOUTH

JUNIOR LITERARY GUILD

NEW YORK

PRINTED AT THE *Country Life Press*, GARDEN CITY, N. Y., U. S. A.

TRANSLATED
FROM THE
RUSSIAN
BY
M. POKROVSKY
ILLUSTRATED
BY
VERA BOCK
19 31

LIST OF ILLUSTRATIONS

OD gave me an excellent memory. I can remember things back to the day of my birth, and as I have seen much, I wish to share some of my recollections with you, my long-nosed and short-nosed friends.

As in most noble crane families, there were two children in ours. My sister and I were born at the same hour, and I distinctly remember the fragments of greenish, brown-speckled egg shells that lay for a while in the bottom of our covert nest.

My first peep at the world puzzled me greatly and

I could scarcely understand anything that was going on around us. But soon my personal experience and the wise teaching of my parents made my surroundings familiar and gave me correct ideas on the events that took place in them—ideas suitable to every decent bird of the crane family that justly holds a position of such prominence in the feathery kingdom.

The time of our arrival in this world was early morning. The sun was still below the horizon, but its golden glow was already reflected in the night fog hanging over the marsh on the border of which about twenty crane families lived.

At first the scenery about our place didn't seem to me a bit attractive. Besides, I felt uncomfortably cold and couldn't help feeling sorry that I was no longer in my former dark, tight dwelling. It had been so warm, and now its wet fragments lay under my weak feet.

All I could see were the hummocks nearest our nest, some small sprigs, and water glittering through the fog somewhere in the distance. Beautiful clouds of gold and rose raced high above our heads and it seemed to me that gay little birds were whistling and chirping right in the midst of them.

As the sun rose it grew much warmer; the fog lifted and disappeared and the magnificent beauty of the sight now revealed to my eyes made me squeak with all my strength in delight.

I saw a wide wonderful plain bounded by the distant horizon. The plain was dotted with lovely hummocks. Some of them were covered with new green shoots of reed and sedge, some hidden beneath a velvety carpet of brownish-red moss, some wreathed by lacy creepers and decked in spring flowers, blue and yellow and white. Here and there sparkled small rivulets and pools and lakes, a few of which were so large that I couldn't see their farther edge.

Bits of white clouds, their shapes constantly changing, floated slowly in the sky, and the very same clouds floated in all the lakes. All sorts of birds, in pairs and flocks, flew about in the air, and the clamor of their shrill cries was such that all their images in the lakes seemed to be echoing the sounds.

Father was not at home. I was told later that he had risen early that morning to go hunting. But Mother was with us and she cleaned our yellow down lovingly with her beak, and one by one straightened our featherless wings that were good for nothing just yet but to flap in delight before the wonders of Nature.

"Well," Mother said to us, "you've stared around long enough, my darlings. Now that you are no longer in your egg cradles where you didn't have to bother about anything, you will have to look about for yourselves and find food to fill your greedy stomachs."

The mention of food made me realize how hungry I was. My sister must have felt hungry, too, for we both opened our yellow mouths wide and squeaked: "Mo-ther! Ea-t!"

"Stop it," said Mother. "I will give you something in a minute. Ours is a country of plenty. But you watch how I get it, so that next time you will know what to do. I don't want to be bothered with you all the time."

Our mother was a kind but practical woman. She always meant well, though sometimes she said things that hurt and used expressions that weren't exactly ladylike. Now she took a few steps to a moss-covered hummock and tore at some of the moss with her beak. We saw several fat worms wriggling appetizingly. My sister and I received equal shares of this delightful food. Mamma had her lunch, too. She

4

swallowed half-a-dozen worms and one little green frog that turned up under her beak.

The warm sun and our full stomachs made us doze dreamily, but a sudden whir of big wings beating the air drove our dreams away.

A great big crane with ash-gray feathers, white breast, shiny black neck and tail, bright red arcs above the brows, and a magnificent tuft on his head swooped down near our nest and said:

"Here I am."

It was our father.

"Oh," he said as he caught sight of us. "Aren't they great! And ugly, I must say! Sons?"

"One is a son, the other a daughter. Look at her! Doesn't she look exactly like her grandmother?" Mother answered, not without pride, and began smoothing our down again.

Father didn't seem to us particularly affectionate at this first meeting, but later we learned to appreciate his true fatherly love that rose at times to heights of heroism. But he was devoid of all sham tenderness and, entrusting our training to the wisdom and experience of his spouse, devoted all his time to social duties.

Now at first acquaintance he only tapped us with his beak as if he counted us, shook his tuft approvingly and, skipping on one spot, shouted to someone,

"We have an increase in the family here!"

In reply to his announcement came the cry, "Congratulations," in a somewhat hoarse voice, and, pushing the sedge aside, another big crane appeared. The newcomer was very old but walked firmly, and bore himself gallantly and with great dignity.

"The early ones," said the guest. And he too tapped us with his beak, adding: "Thank goodness we have a warm spring this year. Everywhere early broods are expected. . . . That means they will be strong enough for the flight across and we shall not suffer such heavy losses in our young stock as last year."

Mother sighed sadly and said:

"Yes, they began to drop one by one from the mouth of the Danube. That was when I lost both of mine. We had to leave my youngest in the Balkan Mountains as he was unable to fly any longer. It was a hard year for us mothers."

What was the "flight across," the "mouth of the Danube," the "Balkan Mountains," and why couldn't last year's youngsters stand something that we were expected to stand? These were all mysteries to us new-born creatures. But at that moment a big black beetle with long feelers, crawling along a grass blade, diverted our attention from the conversation of our elders. We were all eyes, watching the little monster.

The name of the old crane, our neighbor, was Longnose the Wise. He was a bachelor and very fond of children, especially of us as members of the family of his best friend, Clarion Trumpeter, as my father was called.

Longnose would come to our nest several times a day. He helped my mother with her work, chatted about the old days with my father, and in the evening they danced together the farewell greeting to the setting sun. When I woke up occasionally at night I would see our old friend's erect black silhouette standing sentinel for the camp on one of the highest hummocks.

It was not without reason that Longnose was called the Wise. Not alone did he know everything that only highly cultured cranes know, but much more. A long life, extensive travels, a clear mind, and a kind heart, joined to his excellent education had justly won for Longnose his reputation as a wizard. But being of a reserved nature, he never bragged about his achievements, and if he made any mention of his adventures it was always at a fitting moment and in a casual manner, very unlike our other neighbor, the Trifler, who had made only two flights abroad but spoke of them constantly, never missing a chance to tell his audience that he had once perched atop a high minaret in the center of a populous city in Egypt.

Speaking with Longnose once about the night watches that he kept, my father said: "Glory to God, there are no people here, which means that everything is quiet and peaceful."

"There are no people now," replied the Wise One, "but they are sure to come soon. The other day I saw a light cloud of smoke drifting from over there, and yesterday a bullock with a bell about his neck came to the big lake. It means they are near."

"The peasants?"

"Exactly. Shepherds, five men and three pair of dogs."

"Oh, they are harmless," said Mother. "They never carry long-range guns. But farther south live real monsters and cutthroats."

8

"Last year they tried to come up here, but it proved too boggy for them."

All this again sounded mysterious and incomprehensible to us. Soon, however, when we began to stalk on the hummocks and even to make short flights under the guidance of our kind old friend, Longnose the Wise, each day brought us new knowledge. We learned quickly and mysteries vanished.

CHAPTER II

Y COUNTRY was really wonderful! But I'd better proceed to describe it so that you can judge for yourselves.

I said before that the marshy plain where we lived stretched away as far as the eye could follow it; in reality it was even vaster than that. You could fly for three days in any direction and still see the same great hummocked plain, cut here and there by rivers and lakes. The Wise One told us that this plain was called the Great Ostashkovo Marshes.

It was the beginning of summer and all the land was a medley of bright flowers. The velvety meadows contrasted beautifully with the lakes and bogs and served as meeting places for the gay gatherings of all varieties of ducks, geese, plovers, and others of the same brotherhood. Once in a while we also saw some birds that looked a good deal like ourselves, but the resemblance was marked only at a distance. These were herons—wicked, slovenly, greedy birds. They stayed by themselves, trying to keep close to the water, and they knew how to catch silly fish that rose imprudently too near the surface.

Whole settlements of nests lay hidden from sight in all the sheltered places, and everywhere tiny yellow fledglings stirred and squealed. Next to our crane camp was a village of gray ducks and their countless children would frequently visit our camp. We cranes never did them any harm. On the contrary, our watchmen guarded our neighbors as well as ourselves, the ducks being decidedly unfit for regular military service. In the evening when our cranes would flock together to talk, to hold counsel, or to dance the ducks would waddle in from the sedge and join the company. They had one bad trait: they were very fond of gossiping and telling tales about one another.

The Wise One told me that this was their racial weakness. "They are good people, but great hypocrites and tale bearers, and these are grave faults in any decent bird. Thank God, we cranes are free of such failings."

Our days were now run on schedule. We would wake up at dawn and stretch our wings as we skipped on one spot to exercise our already long legs, stiffened during our sleep. Then we would go on a short flight, sometimes with our parents but oftener with our old friend. During these excursions we learned a great deal by observing the things about us and listening to our teacher's explanations. Then we had our luncheon, which was even more enjoyable now than it had been, since there were plenty of huckleberries, red bilberries, and our favorite cranberries which were not quite ripe. Sometimes we would spend the whole day away from home and return only before the beginning of the Dance Council. Our parents were never worried over our long absences, having complete confidence in the prudence and good sense of our preceptor, the Wise One. But Mother always insisted on being told all that we had seen and heard during the day.

Soon we learned to recognize different kinds of danger and to tell our friends from our enemies—a knowledge which is all important in this life! For example, we now knew that such formidable and seemingly ferocious animals as the bull and the cow, with their long sharp horns, were perfectly harmless and that we could almost sit on their backs. But a polecat, so small and pretty, or a beautiful but wicked red fox were arrant murderers and enemies, devouring not only birds' eggs but the birds themselves, especially the fledglings.

"It is for that reason," the Wise One told us, "that, as you have probably noticed, all the birds here build their nests far from firm ground, so that these evildoers may not be able to reach them without drenching their beautiful fur coats in the water and taking the risk of being drowned in the muddy bog."

Then, we learned to know the enemies that were even more dangerous than the polecat and the fox. These were the eagles and vultures. They would soar high in the air above our heads, then swoop down and fly up again, grasping their prey in their claws.

The appearance of these marauders threw all the bird settlements into a panic. The young geese, the teal ducks, and the plover suffered most. Shrill screams, squeaks, and all manner of sounds rent the air. Mothers spread their wings to hide their youngsters. The men hissed threateningly and ruffled their feathers, and our brave cranes loudly trumpeted the alarm, assuming such threatening attitudes that the robbers, seeing all these military preparations, never dared come down.

From the evening talks of the grown-up cranes I gathered that human beings were not to be counted among our friends, and soon I had an opportunity of observing that the birds were not the only ones to suffer from the disfavor of these two-legged animals.

This is how it happened.

Once flying over a big lake, we noticed on one of its sand banks a column of ill-smelling smoke.

"Shall we fly down?" asked my sister timidly.

"Why not?" said the Wise One. "We will alight a little farther in the bushes. From there we shall see everything without exposing ourselves unnecessarily. You can make your observations and draw your conclusions."

THE EAGLES WOULD SOAR HIGH IN THE AIR,
THEN SWOOP DOWN

We alighted in the bushes and were soon in a position to take a good look at a small group of people gathered about a campfire. Their herds of cows and sheep were grazing in the distance. About twenty small, underfed horses stood apart, frantically swishing their tails to drive away the annoying gnats and horseflies.

The people were employed just then in what seemed to me a horrid business. They had just killed a lamb and were skinning it. The red blood spurted on the sand and smeared their hands, clothes, and even their faces. These monsters seemed to be quite happy at their task; they sang and laughed and one of them danced very ungracefully to the tune of his harmonica. Their dogs sat about in a semi-circle, staring intently at the lamb. They must have been very hungry, for their wet red tongues were hanging out.

"Oh, what is it they are doing!" my sister shrieked in horror. "Murderers! They are worse than eagles or vultures!"

"No, not exactly," said the Wise One after a short deliberation. "The people breed their animals, take care of the young, feed them and protect them against the wolves and other dangers. In compensation they make use of their meat and skins. The birds of prey do not work, they take care of nobody and think only of themselves when they seize their victims at random. They live by banditry, the people by what is called their industry. Later, my children, you will learn to know the difference between these two words."

Hardly had he spoken when the dogs caught sight of us and rushed toward us, barking furiously. Naturally, we were very frightened and flew up, leaving our pursuers far behind.

From sunset to dawn swarms of gnats and mosquitoes hung like buzzing clouds above the marshes. They didn't bother us in the least, since we now had our armor of stiff, stratified feathers that no sting could penetrate. But the people, the cows, horses, dogs, and all the fur animals suffered intensely, and when the big gray horseflies appeared in addition to the mosquitoes they all moved somewhere behind the western hills.

We birds remained in sole possession of the great plains and lived undisturbed.

We had grown so that we were almost as big as our parents. There were a great many cranes of our age, and we were a large and joyous company and had wonderful times together. The young geese, ducks, and other fledglings had their feathers too and were no longer funny-looking yellow balls. Enlivened by the stir and bustle of all these frisky youngsters, our marshes seemed much more populous.

We had gradually extended the sphere of our excursions and now we could fly in an hour a distance that formerly we could not have covered in a day. Sometimes we flew so far that we had to stay overnight in a strange place. We learned to sleep, as the saying goes, with one eye open and took turns standing guard. On one such excursion we witnessed a fearfully bloody drama that left a deep impression on our tender hearts.

Tired from the long flight, we had hastily grouped ourselves in a semi-circle and, standing on one foot and tucking the other in, had begun to doze when the shrill trumpets of our sentinels woke us and sent us soaring promptly into the air. Then, by the light of the moon, we saw a large cow galloping heavily along the marshy plain, her terror-crazed calf at her side, pursued by four howling wolves who gnashed their teeth hungrily as they ran. The pursuers were already upon their unfortunate victims, encircling them and cutting off their retreat.

"Why doesn't she run faster?" asked my sister in anguish, but, without waiting for an answer, realized why the cow was moving so slowly. She might still have escaped but she was unwilling to leave her helpless child.

We began to scream and make all sorts of noises to frighten the wolves away, flying about madly in our earnest desire to help the cow. But the cruel beasts never noticed us. They threw themselves on the poor mother, who paused now, ready to accept their challenge. A fierce unequal battle began. Only one of the villains was pierced by the cow's hard horn, while the other three fastened their teeth in her neck and the poor peaceful animal fell to the ground. Then began a barbarous feast, at the sight of which all our feathers stood on end.

"Not so bad," said somebody near us in a harsh voice. "I hope something will be left for me."

It was a big lynx with gleaming eyes and little tassels on his ears. He had come running in our direction, stepping softly as a cat, and now sat watching the fight and waiting for some left-overs from the feast.

"You see," said our teacher, "in this life the same events can be seen from different points of view. A sight that fills us with terror pleases this long-eared scoundrel. The death of one gives life to another. And all this is apparently right and as it should be. Still, I am very glad that we cranes belong to the herb-eating birds. It is so much easier on the conscience!"

"And worms and young frogs?" I thought, remembering our luncheon. But in comparison with the bloody tragedy that had just taken place before our eyes, these worms and young frogs seemed a trifle, not worth mentioning.

CHAPTER III

EFORE we knew it, the summer was almost at an end. The sun rose later and the evening dusk fell earlier every day. The nights were no longer warm, and once, waking up in the morning, we saw our dear hummocks apparently sprinkled with salt. This was the first frost. The gnats, mosquitoes, and flies were gone; only an occasional great gray horsefly, warmed by the noonday sun, would rise in solitary flight.

The smoke from the shepherds' camp fires on the border of our marshes grew to be a daily occurrence, and the air smelt continually of burning leaves. One felt that great changes were about to take place in Nature.

"Autumn, to be followed by a long severe winter, is coming," our friend Longnose told us, and at that evening's conference he proposed the discussion of a possible date for our flight south.

The conference agreed with Longnose that "it was time," but after estimating the fighting strength of our colony, it was resolved to wait for the reinforcements coming from the north, to invite the parties of northern cranes to rest for a few days in our marshes and then to start together for the south.

"Flying in large flocks is preferable in every way," our teacher told us. "In the first place, it is pleasant socially; then it permits more frequent relief to those in responsible positions during the flight, and it has its advantages at the halting places. Sometimes all the convenient resting places are occupied by other travelers. When the caravan is small they simply will not let you come down, whereas when it is large, you can take any place, if necessary, by force."

"When I was in Cairo—that is in Egypt," the Trifler could not help putting in his word—"I was

all alone against thousands of pigeons and swallows sitting on the golden dome of a mosque, but I never hesitated for one moment and———"

"Please don't," my papa stopped him. "We have heard that story more times than there were pigeons and swallows who retreated before your gallant descent upon them."

"I thought this would be a good time to mention it," grumbled the Trifler, and he went to the ducks who were a far readier audience for his stories than were we cranes.

About twenty trustworthy cranes were dispatched to fly in different directions, to scout and to negotiate with the parties of southbound cranes, inviting

them to the general rallying point—our marshes.

As a result of these exertions, in three days there were so many cranes assembled in our marshes that all the hummocks and meadows were closely packed with the representatives of our beautiful race.

The ducks from the neighboring village had left some time before; they fly slowly, so they cannot afford to lose any time.

Double-snipes, snipes, and others of the lesser fry had started even before the ducks, and as we wished them godspeed we promised to catch up with them and to see them very soon.

We were to start at night; for that reason the whole preceding day was spent at home, resting. All the calculations were now completed. The whole army was divided into triangles—thirty cranes in each. The schedule of forepost duties in each triangle and of sentinel watches during the rest periods had been worked out for the entire passage.

We young birds spent the last day at home in eager excitement over the prospect of the long and interesting journey to which we had been looking forward impatiently. We wondered at our elders who dozed peacefully as they waited for the evening dusk and who seemed reluctant to leave the country of their birth. To us it seemed that the last day was infinitely long and that the sun hardly moved, and we felt weary of our once-dear native marshes.

The skies were so red at sunset that the marshes seemed to be aglow with firelight. The air was still. We broke up into triangles, awaiting only the signal to rise. It grew quite dark. Longnose the Wise, who had been unanimously elected Supreme Guide for the entire flight, was in my triangle, the leader of which was our papa, Clarion Trumpeter.

At the very moment when the last glowing ray of the sun vanished into the dark mist beyond the horizon we heard the guide's shrill signal which was immediately answered by hundreds of other trumpets, and my triangle rose gradually, first flying low over the hummocks, then higher and higher, wings beating in a slow, easy rhythm. We flew with our necks somewhat bent, our beaks thrust forward, and our long legs thrown back, trying to keep the line so that those behind us might benefit by the current of air cut by the leaders. This made flying in the rear much easier. So it was only fair that each of us should take his turn flying at the forepost, an arrangement that divided the hardships of flight equally among all.

The higher we rose in the air, the darker seemed the land below. There was only occasionally the glitter of lakes and streams and the dimly gleaming lights of human dwellings, and now and then we heard songs and the barking of dogs and the distant sound of howling that must have come from the throats of wolves trying to approach the cattle. But soon all these sounds ceased, and only the powerful flapping of our wings and the whistling of the cold air as we cut through it broke the stillness of the long autumn night.

It was a solemn moment. We young birds scarcely dared breathe. All our thoughts were concentrated on the flight. To beat our wings in time with the others, to keep the line and the pace of the flight were the only things that now mattered. We flew silently and even the changing of the posts was accomplished in utter silence. The darkness of the night (we could hardly see the farther ends of our own triangle) added to the solemnity of our rhythmic motion. We were at last on our great journey and none of us felt any fatigue. Only at dawn, when the east was growing light, did we notice that our wings were much heavier, that our legs kept their position with difficulty, and that our beaks seemed to have stones tied to their tips and drooped against our wills, pulling our sleepy heads along with them.

It was time to think of a rest, and hearing again the clarion signal of Longnose, we began gliding slowly downward, maintaining our military order all the while, to the new territory that we had never seen before.

I could not decide whether the distance covered during that night was great, and I asked Papa. "And what is your own opinion?" he asked in his turn.

"I think we have done as much as we used to do in the course of a three-day excursion," I said.

"Fine! And that means we have done pretty well for the first stretch," Papa said genially as he looked around. "Well, youngsters, are you tired?"

"Not at all," squeaked my sister, and sticking her head under her left wing and tucking up her right leg she promptly fell asleep, indifferent even to the excellent and almost ripe cranberries that were growing under her very nose.

Eager to see the sights, I looked about, but there was nothing new or different in our first resting place. The scenery seemed to be very much like that in our own neighborhood and I decided to follow my sister's example, but before doing so I thrust my beak left and right into the cranberries, as if I were eating them. This I did in sheer imitation of our older cranes, for I was too sleepy to eat.

29

E DID not sleep long. The sun had just risen above the horizon when we woke up and lazily opened our sleepy eyes, not to close them again for the whole day as there was so much that was new and interesting to see.

We made a short flight and came down to a small marsh near a noisy stream with brilliant green banks that ran through the bushes. A large village was visible near by. The glass windows of the newly built peasant cottages, with their intricate open woodwork and carving, gleamed brightly in the sun. Beyond the village stretched yellow patches of peasant fields with rows of carefully stacked sheaves.

"Such ricks, as those piles of sheaves are called," the Wise One told us, "are well worth sounding with the beak," and we soon learned that this was indeed the case.

Beyond the fields were thickets of various trees— now dark patches of firs, then clumps of birches with their silvery trunks and yellow foliage that was already falling. Still farther away more villages could be seen, and churches with pale green cupolas and golden crosses. The villages were linked by narrow winding roads that ran in all directions. There was one road too that ran perfectly straight; with rows of slender posts at either side connected by wires. We noticed that all the carts running smoothly and noiselessly along the narrow roads began rumbling heavily as soon as they turned into the straight road, and the noise they made frightened us at first.

There were many more people than in our place. The white blouses and red kerchiefs of women were to be seen everywhere. Very close to us—about twenty wing flaps away—a herd was grazing, its bells tinkling. I thoroughly disliked the dirty little shepherd, who seemed to be casting evil glances in our direction as he chewed his bread and dragged his long rope whip behind him.

"It was not quite so crowded last year, was it?" said the Wise One to my father.

"It will be difficult to look after the children in such a commotion," said Mother.

"Let us move," suggested Papa.

The leaders held a conference and the command was given to leave immediately. We flew to the farther bank of the river, passed the birch grove, and came down over a lovely meadow that was less exposed than the first one.

Here we found another of our triangles, the one led by the Trifler. That fellow, as they laughingly told us, had almost lost his head as a result of his pranks. You see, he had heard that all great travelers inscribe their names in places of interest or historical significance. Following their example and profiting by the early-morning hour when people were still asleep, he had gone down, he said, the chimney of the house of the sheriff himself. But the minute he thrust his head in and was about to write his name, heavy clouds of smoke began rising into the chimney.

Suffocated, the Trifler all but fell down in a swoon in the yard where a huge shaggy dog and an old woman with a big stick were waiting for him.

"Still, I wrote the first letter of my name," said the "great traveler" proudly.

Since nobody could verify the truth of his story, it was accepted as authentic.

"May the eagle peck me to death or the crocodile swallow me if this fellow will not ruin the whole triangle some day," said Papa the Clarion.

"And what is a crocodile?" asked my sister.

"A crocodile? Well, you will see one some day," said Papa evasively.

"The crocodile, my pretty one, is such a vile and wicked beast," volunteered one of the older cranes—but here a sudden loud sound reached our ears. There was a flash of fire somewhere among the fir trees and a light smoke rose from their dark branches.

There was no time to finish the story about the crocodiles for we all rose abruptly and flew away, not to come down till we had flown for half an hour to a distance where no dangers threatened us.

"This, my children," said Clarion Trumpeter, speaking to the young cranes, "that you have just

33

heard, is the worst thing in this world. It carries the greatest danger of them all. Is everyone safe?"

Longnose the Wise, who had been taking stock of the situation as he flew, hastened to reassure us.

"Yes, thank goodness!"

"But what was it?" we wanted to know.

"The hunters," said Papa.

"They are men carrying rifles," explained the Wise One, "and I strongly advise you all, when you see them—keep away! Safety first."

"But who was on duty? Whose turn was it?" came resentful inquiries from several of our elders.

The Trifler was revealed as the guilty one and he was punished by so severe a shaking that my sister and I felt sorry for him.

"It is necessary to uphold the strictness of our rules. Discipline is all important when crowds are being handled, and though, fortunately, nobody has actually suffered this time, the punishment is well deserved," said an old crane.

The Trifler shrugged his rumpled wings and, giving the moralizing crane a scornful glance, went to resume his duties as sentinel.

It had been decided to spend all that day and the

following night resting, so that we could fly next day from early morning to sunset.

"Such an arrangement is much better when flying over the populous districts," said our old cranes.

During the day our camp was moved several times, and at dusk we went to the fields where whole rows of ricks remained ungarnered. Devouring the delicious food, we young birds felt some scruples regarding our right to do so, but the old cranes eased our consciences by the assurance that this pillaging was our only revenge upon the people for their constant, inexcusable attempts on our lives.

"Let it be known, gentlemen," announced the Wise One, as he plucked busily at a magnificent barley sheaf, "that people eat us and, more than that, soak us in vinegar as a preliminary."

The night passed quietly.

CHAPTER V

HE sights that we saw on
the third day of our journey
were so striking and un-
usual that I shall never forget them.

We rose before dawn and
flew just over the tops of
the fir trees. At daybreak
we began to rise higher. With every wing beat the
panorama below us grew lovelier. We were passing a
mighty river, on whose banks we saw more churches
and human dwellings than ever before. We also saw
more straight roads, over which moved whole rows of
houses on wheels, with a great monster heading the

procession. The monster had fiery eyes and a long smoky tail. But all this was nothing compared to what we saw at noon.

A big city lay stretched before us. The golden domes of its churches sparkled in the sun and there were so many of them that the city seemed to consist of nothing but churches, one more beautiful than the other. It was built on high hills, and a river spanned by bridges here and there cut it into two almost equal parts. Stone mansions stood in lovely relief against dark garden patches, now in their autumn hues. An intricate net of streets and lanes covered the city. Thousands upon thousands of people crowded the streets and the sound of their voices and the noise of their carriages occasionally reached our ears. But a wonderful, melodious sound, whose faint notes had enchanted us as we were approaching the city, now triumphed over all the other sounds, filling the fresh autumn air so that we seemed to have overtaken its rhythm and to be beating our wings in time to it as we flew. These were the church bells for which our country is so famous.

"Isn't it wonderful! Isn't it beautiful!" my sister kept repeating in ecstasy, half closing her eyes.

But can you imagine my astonishment when I saw our own kind in one of the city squares?—I mean creatures standing exactly like our cranes on one foot, the other tucked underneath! I immediately communicated my discovery to my neighbors in the triangle, and the news went farther until it reached my papa, and despite the church bells I heard his roar of laughter and the Wise One's comment.

"Those are not cranes, but soldiers!"

"What are soldiers?" we asked.

"Soldiers are people with rifles, but rifles not so dangerous for us birds as those of the hunters."

"But why do they stand like cranes?" my little sister was curious to know.

"Good examples will always find imitators." Thus did the Wise One settle the question.

At that moment we were passing over the very center of the city, whose name our wise teacher had told us. In spite of my excellent memory I have forgotten it, but I shall try to describe some of its more important characteristics, by which you will probably recognize it.

The hill in the heart of the city was encircled by a wide indented wall with several towers descending

THE GOLDEN DOMES OF ITS CHURCHES SPARKLED
IN THE SUN

almost to the very river. The slopes between the wall and the river were covered with bright green lawns and trees. Behind the wall, in the center of the enclosure, stood a big house with a golden roof, and about this house rose the domes of the countless churches, one of which was the highest in the whole city. It was from the belfry of that church that the loudest bell boomed forth its basso, drowning the sounds of all the other bells exactly as our papa, the Clarion Trumpeter, does at the conference when he wants to make the others listen to him.

Great as the city was, it did not take us long to fly over it, and since we didn't come down till dusk, we saw more cities and more wonderful things that day. When I compared all I had seen with our native marshes—why, there simply was no comparison, for our melancholy marshland fell far below the mark! Everyone talks of the "mother country," but what is a mother country? An accidental place chosen by blind chance. Why then should it be so dear? Every spot, every little thing here was so much gayer and more beautiful that I couldn't understand all the fuss that was made about one's birthplace.

"You will understand later," said one of our old cranes.

His remark made me feel ashamed of myself. Not only was I thinking aloud, but something inside me told me that my thinking was all wrong and even silly.

CHAPTER VI

HE stretch that we covered
that day seemed to us much
shorter than any previous
one, but it seemed so only
because all the interesting
things we saw made us forget time and space. We
came down toward eve-
ning over a wide meadow among the aspen woods.
Utter silence reigned here.

The nearest habitation, as reported by our scouts,
was about two miles away and the aspen trees completely screened us from the side of the road. A
stream ran through the meadow, and the minute our

triangle descended, flocks of plovers who had settled there for the night rose excitedly from its banks.

Papa hastened to reassure them, inviting them to stay with us overnight and sleep quietly under our protection. The invitation was enthusiastically accepted by these little folk, who were profuse in their expressions of gratitude.

"We never expected to catch up with you so soon. We thought we should meet you much farther south," Longnose said to them.

"What's the use of hurrying?" replied one of the plovers. "The weather is still quite warm and worms are abundant everywhere, so we take our time."

"I don't think you're wise," our leader commented disapprovingly. "The frosts may come while you linger here. What will you do then? You'll all freeze to death. Where do you come from?"

A plover told him some name. Longnose appeared greatly surprised.

"So! We passed there only yesterday. And how long is it since you started?"

"This is the sixth day. You know we cannot go fast."

"Still, you'd better hurry—though you don't go

44

as far as we do," said our Papa, eying our flock proudly as if he were comparing it with that of our neighbors. "I know you usually winter at the mouth of the Danube, but if you don't hurry I'm afraid the frost will catch you in the steppes."

"Yes, please do be quick," the Trifler put in; "the bustards once met with such a terrible accident. I didn't actually see it myself, but I've heard about it."

"What are bustards?" questioned my sister.

"They are birds, my dear, migratory birds. Well, these bustards once happened to be in a very unfortunate position, for a sudden frost had caught them. It had rained all night, you see, and was very warm and the bustards were soaked to their marrow, yet they slept. In the morning came a terrible frost. Their wings were frozen and covered with ice so that they couldn't move them and suddenly some shepherds appeared——"

"Heavens!" ejaculated several listeners in agitation.

"The bustards tried to run away, but who can run fast with frozen wings? And they were all caught alive!"

"Poor devils!"

"The most atrocious kind of slaughter was raging and if I had not——"

"How is that, if you never actually saw it yourself?" chuckled Papa.

"Did I say 'I'? I meant to say if it hadn't been for the sun that rose and thawed the bustards' frozen wings, all the flock would have perished. I was told about this accident, or rather, my uncle-cousin was told about it—you doubtless remember him, the famous Crack Dancer who spent two years in captivity with human beings and despite the weekly clipping of his wings managed to escape, disguising himself as a dog——"

Here even we children understood that the storyteller had lost himself in the labyrinth of his lies, and we replied with an outburst of laughter that was echoed by the open spaces somewhere beyond the aspen woods now shadowed from our sight by the night mist.

"Sleep!" sounded the signal of our guide. "Sleep!" answered the leaders of the triangles from here and there.

"Yes, sir!" replied ten-score voices, and ten-score

noses were buried beneath left wings as we plunged into sweet dreams of a roseate future.

"Hear!" came the cry from the sentinels' quarters.

"Hear!" repeated the echo near the fir trees. "Hear!" rose a faint sound from afar, and then close by it began all over again.

These were our vigilant sentinels, faithful to their duties.

CHAPTER VII

T WAS still dark when I was awakened by Longnose issuing an order, whose last words gave me a pleasant thrill.

"Be sure to return promptly so that we can reach the peas before sunrise. The flight shouldn't take more than half an hour. Be careful and keep your eyes wide open."

My little sister had also heard the word "peas," and she smacked her lips in her sleep. I must say my own mouth began to water.

"The peas! At last!" We had heard so much about

the delectable qualities of that food, yet had never had a chance to taste it. Now we were assured of this long-desired delicacy by our wise leader's order.

It was easy to understand that neither my sister nor I could sleep any longer.

I watched two reconnoitering squads, one of three, the other of five cranes, rise and disappear in the darkness. Both squads flew in the same direction.

The tireless Trifler started after them.

"You'd better stay," Papa shouted to him.

"I'm afraid they'll get it all mixed up," replied our volunteer.

"Be careful, you don't get mixed up."

My sister whispered into my ear: "You remember, Mama said 'this' tastes better than barley."

"You know what I'll do," I said. "I'll eat and eat and eat, as long as I can, then I'll stock myself up— I mean I'll fill my mouth behind the cheeks. What do you think it looks like?"

While we were speculating on how the peas looked and tasted, one of the reconnoitering squads came back.

They reported that this year the peas were planted much closer to the village, but were well screened from view by the large hay ricks, so that if we got there early we could have all the peas we wanted before sunrise.

Then the other party of scouts came back.

"Where is the Trifler?" Papa asked anxiously.

"He said he would stay there and watch until you came."

"Oh dear, he'll get into trouble," the Wise One thought aloud. "Take off!" he commanded.

Noiselessly as we rose, still our flight frightened the slumbering plovers. We set off in small parties, since it wasn't worth forming into triangles for so short a flight.

Soon the smell of manure and chimney smoke told us we were in the proximity of human settlements.

The dark outlines of the peasant cottages were hardly perceptible on the horizon; near us loomed some large dark masses.

"Those are the hayricks," said one of the scouts in a low voice to Papa as he led the way for our party. "Here, gentlemen, to your left!"

We were descending. Then my legs were entwined in something soft and clinging, and I stuck my nose into the ground.

"Careful!" said Papa as he came to my assistance. "That is it."

"What 'it'?"

My heart was beating fast. I hastened to disentangle my legs.

"Peas."

Yes, those were peas! and it was something that surpassed even our expectations. The long intertwined stalks of this wonderful plant were loaded with ripe pods full of excellent, sweet pea kernels, with an occasional small worm that tasted even better than the peas!

As we all fell to, the air was filled with the lively sound of the opening of pods and the rustle of stalks.

"No gulping. Take your time," Longnose instructed us. "There is plenty of time before sunrise. The people and their dogs are still asleep."

Our leader himself was standing watch for us. As he stood on top of a hayrick we could all see his graceful silhouette outlined against the pale skies. With such a guard one could certainly enjoy in safety the gifts of Nature!

Only the absence of the Trifler caused us some anxiety and marred our blissful mood. We looked for him and even tried to call him, but there was no response from the darkness.

Suddenly we heard his scream from the direction of the village. It was a scream of mortal agony and terror. Yes—there was no doubt! We recognized the voice of our heedless friend.

An alarm signal was given from the hayrick and the whole crane flock promptly set out in disorder after my Papa who shouted: "Here, follow me!"

We flew over the ravine, through whose bed a brook flowed, and hid ourselves in the brushwood.

Meantime, daylight began to glimmer. Since we were now in a relatively safe place, we decided to wait until morning, when we might possibly learn something of our dear friend's fate. Naturally, we couldn't leave him without at least making an attempt to help him.

The sleepy village was now in a state of commotion. Lights appeared here and there at the windows, the dogs were barking loudly, calling to one another and gathering in groups. The gates creaked as they opened and cows and horses appeared, stepping heavily over the gate boards. Black curly sheep, looking very much like balls, seemed to roll out into the street, bleating cheerfully. Smoke clouds rose from the chimneys, well wheels squeaked, and children and women came out muffling themselves in their sheepskins and yawning lazily behind their hands.

When it grew quite light we sent two experienced and sharp-eyed cranes to fly over the village and spy on what was going on there.

They went and stopped motionless high, high in the air, hovering above the center of the village. We could see them well, as the sun's rays lit them from below. Now they circled around, then descended some distance and flew over a village street; they seemed to be flying so low that we feared for their safety. Then they soared up and came down again in another part of the village, doing the same thing over and over again. Finally they turned back.

What would they have to say?

Exactly what had happened to the poor Trifler our scouts could not tell. But they had seen a big crowd assembled in front of the priest's house and had heard someone shouting from the shed for a cord and scissors.

"Bad business," said an old crane.

"No escape," agreed another.

"My dear friends," said our guide sadly but firmly, "we cannot lose any more time. The fate of our dear, careless friend now lies entirely in the hands of God. We cannot do a thing. Let us profit by this cruel lesson and learn to think before we act. Now into triangles! God be with us!"

And we set forth with heavy hearts and stomachs overstuffed with peas, and we thought of the frailty of earthly happiness in general—and that of the cranes in particular.

CHAPTER VIII

 E FLEW all day in a state of great depression. The accident to our friend the Trifler was the first mishap of our journey that until then had gone so happily and smoothly.

As if to make matters worse the weather changed. Dark clouds from the north drew closer in pursuit, gray mist covered the region, and it began to rain. The landscape below was as cheerless as the weather; there were endless patches of cropped fields and winter fallow. Several times before we had been lucky enough to outstrip the

55

clouds and reach the sunlit spaces, warming our wet, stiff wings and legs in the sun's rays. But this time all the skies were leaden gray and there was no prospect of a change in the weather when at the end of the day we descended wearily for the night rest to a large yellowish meadow near a swampy thicket, in the shelter of whose outskirts lay a few shabby peasant huts.

But imagine our amazement and joy when, as we glided down to the meadow, we saw our Trifler strolling beside the hedge and gazing upward as if watching for our arrival!

"You! You should be thrashed!" Our leader fell upon him.

"Of course he should be," agreed Papa.

"Why?" asked the Trifler, shrugging his wet wings.

"Why! For the trouble you gave us all!"

"Believe me, my friends, I had more trouble than you," said the Trifler.

"Really? Tell us what happened to you! Where have you been all this time?"

"Oh, that's quite a story. I shall certainly tell you all about it, but not now, all at once. I want you to rest and make yourselves comfortable, and then, my friends, I shall ask for your attention." And the Trifler, tossing his head high, ran his eyes over the assemblage.

"Yes, ladies and gentlemen, what happened to me was altogether unusual, and it is only owing to my experience and my presence of mind, together with an extraordinary stroke of luck, that I am now with you again instead of pining in captivity, my wings all but chopped off, for the diversion of dirty village boys——"

"Tell us quickly all about it!" my dear sister shrieked impatiently.

But the Trifler would not be persuaded and only after we had rested, shaken out and arranged our feathers, and formed in a circle did the Trifler step into its center and, after some posturing, begin his tale.

"Ladies and gentlemen! While you were enjoying the peas—for I must own I do not care for that stuff, especially when the dates and cocoanuts——"

"What are they?" my sister queried.

"Don't interrupt!" and I nudged her in the side.

The speaker eyed us silently so that we both blushed.

57

"So—while you enjoyed the peas, I went for a walk through the village. I love to study the manners and customs of people and such animals and it was solely for that purpose that I looked into their yards and even into their windows. I noticed that one of them was half open and was attracted by a lovely smell of freshly baked bread. I came nearer, stuck my head into the window and looked around. The cottage was dark inside and I heard the snoring and breathing of several sleeping persons. The tiniest pigs were grunting and stirring near the stove. On the table quite near me lay a whole loaf of bread covered with a clean towel, a fancy wooden salt box, and several carved spoons scattered here and there. I thought of taking one of them as a souvenir——"

"In other words, you wanted to steal it!" Longnose reproved him sternly.

"To steal! What an expression! When Englishmen took the whole Cleopatra's Needle from Egypt nobody ever thought of applying such a word to their action!" the Trifler retorted. "And what is a wooden spoon compared to a stone obelisk?"

"Go on," nodded Papa.

"Very well, then! To reach the spoon I had to stick

my neck in a little farther. As I seized the spoon the wretched window suddenly fell down, crushing my neck——"

"Oh Lord! Oh Lord!" we exclaimed.

"The pain was simply unbearable. I thought my neck was broken in two. Crazed by the pain, I yelled at the top of my lungs and began beating my wings and struggling in an effort to break away. The glass fell out of the window and its noise awakened the people in the cottage. A dog, barking, and yelping, was trying to get at my tail and legs, but I was kicking so violently that he couldn't come near me.

"Meantime they brought a light to the window.

" 'Oh, that's what it is!' 'Catch him, take him, kill him!' cried various voices.

" 'Why kill him? Take him alive,' another voice interposed in my behalf.

"I was instantly seized from behind, released from the window's clutches but held tightly between someone's knees, and my head was covered with a dirty sack. I was a prisoner.

"From the acute pain in my neck, the lack of air, and the earlier exhausting struggle, I fainted, and recovered my senses only a few minutes later to discover that someone was carrying me and that I was the subject of lively discussion and argument.

" 'Take him to the priest. He will give us some vodka for him.'

" 'Yes, that's a good idea. He has one already, so this one will be company for him.'

" 'Imagine the bird's impudence! First I took him for a wood demon, but no! A bird looking into people's windows!'

" 'Oh dear, oh dear, didn't he scare me out of my wits!' A peasant woman yelled. 'My feet grew stiff, I couldn't move nor call for help, curse him, the bird!'

" 'Antipka! Vanka! Grunka! Come here quick!— they have caught a cranny!' called the voices of children.

" 'Maybe it is the priest's?'

" 'No, a wild one!'

"Then some gate creaked, the sack was removed from my head, and I was on my feet again. Exhausted and unhappy as I was, still I was interested in my new surroundings and I gazed about me. I was in a spacious shed, whose door had just closed behind me. There were several barrels and tubs, some boxes, a baby carriage without wheels, some crockery, and horse collars and harness hanging on the wall.

" 'Hello, friend!' said a voice.

"I shuddered and looked in the direction from which this friendly greeting came. You can imagine my surprise and joy to see a crane of our breed looking quietly and rather sadly into my eyes!

" 'You are caught, my poor Brother,' he said, shaking his head.

" 'But how is it that you are here?'

" 'It is three years since they found me in the woods and brought me here. I was taken ill and couldn't follow my triangle in its flight across.'

" 'Couldn't you escape?'

" 'Escape! My wings are clipped. One cannot walk very far. They will clip yours too; you'll see how it feels!' said my melancholy host.

"The world swam before my eyes; I felt dizzy. Only the voices behind the door brought me back to reality.

" 'Where is that new cranny?' somebody asked.

" 'Here, little Father, in the shed. It is together with yours, and they look so much alike!'

" 'I have an excellent idea, my friend,' my fellow prisoner spoke hastily. 'They will be here in a minute. They are sure to clip your wings. Do as I tell you and you will be saved.'

" 'Saved—if only I could be!'

" 'Well, when they enter you stay where you are and act like a tame bird and I will be wild. You understand?'

" 'I do.'

"The door opened and the people began coming in. The first to enter was an old man in a long gray under-cassock, his hair tightly braided behind; this was the village priest. He was followed by two peasants with red beards, behind whom several heads were visible, with hats and without, then the bright head-kerchiefs of women and the flaxen heads of children.

"The entrance was shadowed by all these spectators and the interior of the shed was in semi-darkness. My savior was running wildly around the shed, beating his wings, while I, following his advice, sat quietly on a barrel and watched the proceedings.

" 'Here is my darling,' said the priest, stroking my head. I never moved.

" 'Catch him, catch him, lads! Drive him to the corner!' 'Isn't he nimble footed! You can see at once how wild he is.'

"My chivalrous friend was struggling desperately to escape the hands of his pursuers.

" 'Good Lord!' cried the priest when he saw my friend cornered at last. 'Hey, somebody there! Arishka, run into the house! Get me a cord and a pair of scissors.'

" 'Now escape!' groaned my noble brother crane.

"The moment was favorable and no time was to be lost. The enemy was busy with their 'new' prisoner and nobody paid any attention to me. The door of the shed was open. In two leaps I was out of the shed and, almost knocking down Arishka, who was back with the cord and scissors, I rose into the air.

" 'Good-bye, friend!' I shouted to my savior. 'Your name will be entered into the annals of history.'

"I would like to have seen their faces when they saw me flying high in the air and realized what had happened!

"But I flew without looking back. Never in my

life had I attained such speed. If you had seen me you would have taken me for a swallow or an eagle at least, rather than a crane. First I nearly smashed my head against a fir tree. Then, rising higher, I overtook a cloud and shattered it to pieces, and still I flew and flew. But please don't think it was fear that drove me. What nonsense! Fear is unknown to the crane in general and to me in particular. So far as I was concerned, I would gladly have stayed longer in the village to watch further developments, but I thought of you, of your natural anxiety on my account, and I started to catch up with you. One thing I cannot understand is how I could have outstripped you without noticing you. What route did you take?"

Concluding his tale with this question put in a deliberately indifferent manner, the Trifler cast his eyes over the company.

"It was a great and heroic deed," said Longnose the Wise.

"A glorious deed, worthy of our noble and great-hearted race," Clarion Trumpeter agreed.

"I really think," drawled the Trifler, all puffed up, "that you doubt my story and are making fun of

IN TWO LEAPS I WAS OUT OF THE SHED

me." The poor fellow thought that the complimentary remarks were meant for him.

"Nobody's talking about you," our Elder reproved him. "You're only a heedless fool with wonderful luck. We're speaking of the other. You said it was three years since he has been in captivity?"

"Three years," the confused Trifler echoed in a low whisper.

"Oh, let us go back and rescue him!" exclaimed my kind-hearted sister.

All the young birds immediately joined in her plea.

"To rescue him!" Longnose repeated sadly. "A crane with clipped wings has no use for his freedom. He cannot live without the protection of man."

"Besides, he is very valuable to the village community," interposed the Trifler, regaining his usual self-confidence. "It is not without reason that he lives with the priest. He sets a good example to the people, and he told me confidentially that he even composes all the sermons, and the Father has only to learn them by heart and pass them off as his own."

"Lying again! You're hopeless!" Papa stopped him. "Now, my children, let us do a solemn dance in honor of our heroic fellow crane. Fall in! Begin!" he commanded.

And drawing up in a line, we performed the most elaborate of our dances, despite the annoying cold rain that had evidently set in for the entire night.

Under the pretext of fatigue, the Trifler excused himself from taking part in this, our traditional expression of a solemn mood.

CHAPTER IX

I T CLEARED only towards morning. Then a strong, cold wind arose and the terrible incident of the bustards returned to our minds. We simply had to move about to get warm and exercise our stiff wings that refused to serve us properly. Besides, there was absolutely nothing to eat in that place. The few scanty fields surrounding a wretched hamlet had long ago been stripped bare, and as far as the eye could reach there wasn't a thing worth while in sight.

Our excellent guides reassured us, saying that we

69

should soon pass into more fertile regions, so we were only too glad to go.

As we proceeded southward the scenery changed. The dark green fir woods, so dear to our hearts, were no longer in evidence, and even the beauty of our north—the birch—was seldom seen. In their stead dense oak forests, clad now in all their autumn finery, lay stretched below. It was a harmony in golden yellow, flame red, and old bronze. The bright green carpets of wet meadows, dotted by the scarlet of late flowers, were visible in the woods here and there. The roads were no longer dusty and gray—they were wide, oily black tracks, and strings of carts drawn by gray, sharp-horned oxen moved

along them. The people driving the carts wore sheepskin caps, white shirts, and trousers of unusual width. Almost every one of them had a pipe in his mouth and the carts moved slowly and lazily over the sticky black mud of the road.

The villages too that we encountered now were different from those we had seen before. Here they had no gay-looking log cabins with high ridge poles and lacy wood carvings above the cornices. There were no sharp-pointed fences surrounding them and no squeaky gates trimmed with rows of bright nail heads.

The human dwellings here were low mud huts with whitewashed walls, tiny windows, and over-hanging thatched roofs.

71

On the benches beneath the windows sat gray-bearded old men leaning on their walking sticks. Swarthy children ran about. Some of them were playing with knuckle bones, the others were wading through the sparkling rain pools. Near the wells crowded the women, as talkative as everywhere along our flight. At some distance stood a row of windmills, their weatherbeaten arms whirling threateningly. Wagons loaded with white bags stood close by and the unharnessed oxen dozed lazily, chewing their cud. Acres and acres of golden corn stacks surrounded these villages. Farther away stretched endless stubble and freshly tilled fields, the plows being dragged by oxen that looked to us like faint specks.

And the rich soil of the fields, the incessant whirling of the windmills, the acres of golden corn stacks, and even the dogged sluggishness of the people's movements—all spoke of abundance, prosperity, and leisure.

"It certainly looks as if there should be enough for us to share in these riches," Papa said, and he consulted with the leaders of the neighboring triangles.

They decided to descend to the stubbles at a good distance from the village, where one might expect to find plenty of neglected sheafs, separate ears, and loose grains of wheat.

Beating our wings noisily and merrily, and trumpeting our rest signals, we glided down and immediately began feasting.

The Trifler alone seemed to feel out of sorts. He told us none of his usual stories and, after having thrust his beak into the ground a few times, crouched on the hedge, stretching out his long legs.

"You aren't sick, are you?" And our thoughtful Mama approached him.

"I'm afraid something is wrong with my leg," the Trifler replied, "and my neck aches terribly. I can't turn my head."

"That comes from the window that hit you," somebody said.

"That must be it. I didn't feel it so badly in the first excitement and hurry, but now—goodness how it hurts! And look, isn't it swollen?"

We all gathered around our poor Trifler; we all sympathized with him but none of us had any idea what to do to relieve his sufferings.

73

"Don't you get sick," Longnose said to him. "If you stay behind you will perish."

"That's what worries me. But merciful is the Lord! If only the weather would stay warm!"

Our elders decided that, to spare him the strain of the foreposts, the Trifler should fly in the rear from now on. Then Longnose the Wise drew close to the Trifler and scrutinized him for a few long minutes.

The latter assumed such a dejected attitude that I felt like crying with compassion for him.

Then our leader took Papa aside and they began to discuss something, casting occasional glances at our invalid. It was clear enough that he was the subject of their consultation.

My curious little sister, pretending to be picking up some scattered grains, stole near the pair, then rushed back to tell us the news, her eyes sparkling.

"Everything is fine." She spoke hastily. "Longnose said that the trouble with your neck and leg wasn't serious. Though they ache, they will be all right in a few days. It would have been different if your wings had been hurt, he said. Now for your sake they want to do shorter stretches and have longer rests. Longnose said too that we had done so much already that it wouldn't hurt us to go slowly now."

"Stop tattling like a magpie," said Papa, joining our group and tapping my sister on the back of her head.

"Oh, Papa! It hurts!" my sister screamed angrily. "Me a magpie! And you, you are an old sparrow!" We all burst into laughter, the comparison of a crane so tall, stately and beautiful as our Papa with a sparrow seemed so absurd.

My sister was the darling of us all and she was excused for doing many things that were at variance with our rigid discipline.

During this halt we had met a pair of beautiful storks. They were lovely, long-legged, long-nosed white birds with black tails and black edging on their wings and bright red beaks and legs. Their nest was near the chimney on the roof of a house at the edge of the village. They were of the same age as my sister and I and they too were preparing for their first flight south. They were the only two of the whole colony of storks living in the neighborhood to come and make the acquaintance of the "distinguished foreigners," as they called us.

They were really very nice, well-bred birds. The only discordant note in our friendly conversation was their assertion that people are perfectly peaceful and even charming animals who live on very cordial terms with the storks. They told us too that the storks mostly build their nests on the roofs of human habitations, on the cupolas and crosses of their churches, seeking the sides most exposed to the sun.

"We hate the nasty damp shadows," they said.

"Don't the people eat you?" one of our cranes asked.

"And don't they pickle you to make your meat tastier?" another continued.

"Oh, never!" one of the storks denied emphatically. "They have great respect for us and would never even think of such a thing—then, too, they feel under obligation to us for all the services that we render them and are thankful that we never cause them any loss."

"What exactly are the services that you render?" I became interested.

"We destroy all the nasty things that come near their houses, we kill snakes——"

"We never touch their cornfields——"

"That means you have no taste for the good things," remarked our invalid sarcastically as he skipped nearer us.

"Every one to his taste," one of the storks said with a polite bow. "But in any case your prejudice against the people is ill-founded. We walk freely along their streets, even their dogs never touch us. Nobody molests our nests and they even repair them when they get out of order during our absence in winter. And early in spring when we come back—oh, you should see how jubilant they are! The way they greet our homecoming, one would think it was a sort of holiday for them."

"You are one thing—we another," said Papa, who up to then hadn't uttered a single word.

"Let me tell you something." The Trifler suddenly gave vent to his irritation. He was in a peevish mood and determined to take the conceited stork down a peg. "There is no doubt that you, gentlemen, help the people in a certain way. But that is not the point. The people are selfish and clearly not inclined to gratitude. The safety you enjoy you owe to human selfishness."

"How is that?"

77

"Why, it's very obvious! You storks live on all sorts of trash and it makes your flesh taste so—pardon the expression—that the devil himself wouldn't care for it. Whereas our flesh, thanks to our vegetable diet, if it is pickled and properly cooked, makes a remarkable delicacy, and for that reason——"

"You seem to be proud that your flesh suits somebody's stomach!" And the stork shrugged his wings contemptuously.

"What a thing to boast of indeed!" another added.

"I am not boasting, but explaining certain laws that operate in this life. I am trying to show you the foundations of your friendship with the people and of your safety. Everything has a reason. Take daws for example. What on earth can be more contemptible than those birds? And yet they too live very happily under one roof with human beings."

Here Papa noticed that the conversation was taking a dangerous personal turn and he intervened.

"Don't forget, gentlemen, that the noble storks are our guests for the moment——"

If they had only let him, Papa would undoubtedly have said something very fitting and clever, but one of the storks quibbled at the word "guests."

"How is that, if you please?" he flashed. "I should say that you are temporary guests here and we are the hosts. Do you happen to know that all the land about this region belongs to our village?"

"Let us not argue, gentlemen"—it was Longnose who saved the situation—"but recognizing the undeniable rights of the Messrs. Storks over these lands, beg them not to begrudge us their hospitality and allow us to finish our rest quietly. I hope you don't mind, gentlemen?"

"Oh, certainly not," answered the storks, content with the new turn in the affair, and flattered by Longnose's words. "We are getting ready for our journey too."

"To Cairo?"

"Yes, and probably farther."

"In our footsteps?"

"We have our own routes to follow. Good-bye, gentlemen, godspeed!"

"Good-bye."

When the storks were out of sight Papa grumbled: "Make off," and then added angrily: "Isn't it too bad we couldn't teach those fops a good lesson!"

"It would be dangerous," Longnose said.

"If only I were strong enough!" the Trifler was wrathful.

"It would be dangerous," continued our illustrious leader, "because, if we should so much as touch one of these youngsters a huge flock would gather in their defense and we would be challenged to a real fight with unequal forces."

"Besides, my illness—it weakens our forces considerably," the Trifler put in.

"Probably," Longnose smiled. "But more important is the fact that the stork's beaks are longer and stronger than ours. Then, believe me, my friends, the wisest rule for the strong of this earth to follow is to avoid war when peace can be made, even a bad peace. Now let us start."

When we rose in the air the whole surface of the large village and its environs was seen quite distinctly. A great flock of storks was gathering near the windmills. There was much excitement and stir and their warlike shrieks reached our ears.

"It seems we started just in time," said Mama. "Look at them! What a horde!"

The Trifler, who was flying in the rear, turned his head nervously every minute, and began urging those at the foreposts to hurry. Illness shakes the courage, and our hero was beginning to show the white feather.

Shortly before sunset we saw a mighty river glittering below. One of its banks was rocky and steep; the other, almost on a level with the surface of the water, lay buried beneath the dense growth of woods. Hundreds of bays and shallows, their borders thick with reeds and aspens, sparkled against this dark background. Long sandbanks extended on every side and were alive with huge flocks of ducks, wild geese, plovers, and other small waterfowl.

"Hey, children! This is the Dnieper," Papa the Clarion shouted to us. "Look at all the migrating brothers assembled here! This is one of their principal haunts. We too shall stay here to-night and all day to-morrow."

"Halt!" Longnose confirmed the statement.

"Halt! Halt!" the word rang merrily through the triangle and echoed in all the others.

CHAPTER X

H, MY! With what an un-
believable clamor, cackling,
squeaking, and clucking the
innumerable birds of pas-
sage assembled on the river
shoal greeted our arrival!

Thousands of gray teal
occupied the reeds; in a
lagoon wild geese were swimming; black grebes and
divers roamed about, diving deep after the fish. Long-
legged plovers bustled in the sand and ran through
the puddles of water. To the right, near a hollow old
bending willow, stood the broods of surly-looking
spoonbills. Somewhat farther away in the thickness

of the sedge grass, the bitterns boomed, recalling the bellow of an ox. It is simply impossible to name all the breeds represented there!

As we did not want to disturb those who had arrived before us, we took possession of a dry meadow covered with mossy hummocks, about ten rods from the water. There were plenty of blackberries, which we found very much to our liking, and also some acorns. The latter, if they were not so hard, would make a very nice food. But since we had something better, we just tried them to satisfy our curiosity.

From our meadow we could see not only the entire bird camp but also a considerable part of the river, where a heavily laden boat with a sail was moving along. Some people were visible aboard the boat, but they were so far from us that we could watch them without fear. As the place where we camped was in a hollow, closely surrounded by thickets, the problem of the night watchmen was a difficult one and their number was increased.

My sister and I were among those on duty that night, and though she was very sleepy, her sense of duty and responsibility were stronger than her sleepiness. All the instructions had been given, and the plan of the sentinels' positions had been worked out while it was still daylight, so that we might make ourselves familiar with the locality and arrangement of our camp.

With sunset the chattering and noise in the camp ceased, and a dense fog hid from our sight not only the distant rocky bank of the river, but also the oak woods nearest us.

The air was full of incomprehensible noises that sounded mournful, foreshadowing some mortal danger. Perhaps it only seemed so to me, since this was my first night watch.

My sister, whose post was next to mine, suddenly appeared at my side.

"Why, how can you leave your post?" I asked.

"I'm afraid to be alone," she admitted frankly.

At about midnight the fog lifted and we could see the dark starry sky. The night was very cold.

The majestic river was flowing before us once more and even its farther bank was dimly visible.

Presently I noticed some dark objects flowing down the river. Hard as I tried to see what they were, I could distinguish nothing that aroused my suspicions.

They were simply masses of reed and brushwood carried away by the current. But where did they come
from? And why, if they were being carried by the
current, should they turn to the left bank where the
geese and ducks were sleeping?

I told my sister of my doubts; she shared them fully
and suggested calling Papa or one of the older cranes,
starting off immediately to do so.

This seemed to me the best way out. Indeed, we
couldn't sound the alarm before we knew what the
dark objects were. If they were only masses of reed
and the alarm proved false, what a laughing stock
they would make of us!

Papa came instantly to my post. He looked at the
approaching masses with visible dismay.

"I know what it is," he muttered. "Alarm!" And
he was the first to trumpet, seconded by our sentinels.

The sound of our trumpet calls had not yet died
away before fire flashed from the suspicious-looking
floating masses and puffs of smoke appeared.

Goodness knows what followed then. "Hunters!
Hunters!" the birds shouted despairingly in mortal
anguish. And the whole sleepy camp rose with a

deafening noise and flapping of wings and rushed into the woods near by.

We rose too and flew over the woods. Now we could see everything clearly. Three boats, cleverly concealed in the brushwood, had stolen close to the camp. The hunters sitting in the boats were firing mercilessly at the dense flocks of ducks that flew madly about the place!

The wounded and killed fell noiselessly into the water, leaving bloody, floating circles on its surface. Scores of slaughtered ducks were carried away by the current driven toward the shoals. A large gray goose, shot through the wing, was struggling desperately toward a thicket, but another shot struck him and, moaning plaintively, he turned in the air and fell heavily to the ground. But the hunters continued to fire.

At last the ducks understood that their only escape lay in the woods and they all flew in that direction. The firing ceased.

Then the hunters began to pick up their trophies and pile them in the boats. And though many of their victims were carried away by the current and many remained undiscovered in the sedge, their boats were filled to the brim. It was a fearful, ruthless slaughter.

Now the hunters came to shore and built a camp fire. They were lighted up by the red glare and we could see one of them dressing a poor teal duck and putting it on a spit, while another brought some water to boil. Others of the party bathed meantime.

We watched them as we circled high in the air above their heads.

"Let's get away from here," several faltering voices sounded.

"Away? Where?" said Papa disapprovingly. "We are safe here, but who knows? We may fly away and come down only to get into more trouble."

And so it seemed. Farther down the river the fire flamed again. It was another party of hunters attacking another camp of emigrants.

More victims, more blood!

The day began to break. We flew to the rocky bank of the river, leaving a detachment of our cranes to watch the enemy. The latter, after a swim in the river, had their breakfast, talking and laughing merrily; then they returned to their boats and rowed in the direction of what seemed to be a very pretty town surrounded by orchards.

Our elders held a conference and decided that we should go back to our camp. "It is quite safe now," Longnose explained to us. "The hunters are sure that the game frightened away by their attack will never return."

We reached our camp shortly before sunrise; the place now looked like a battlefield.

"Come here!" Papa called to me. "You come too," he said to my sister. Immediately feeling guilty, we both approached him. I thought, however, that I had done my duty that night and my mind was easy on that score.

Papa took us aside, so that the others couldn't hear what he said.

"You see, children, what it is to lose time when you should act? If you had sounded the alarm the minute you noticed the suspicious-looking objects floating in the river, the hunters would have been fooled and there would have been no bloodshed. Instead, you began to wonder and debate and went after me and wasted precious moments."

"Papa," I said, "I was afraid to sound a false alarm. Think of the jeers——"

"Jeers! There's no harm in them. They would certainly have made fun of you, but what of it? They'd get over it. And now, look at all the widows and or-phans——"

"Papa, all ours are safe," I interposed.

"Ours!" Papa mimicked me, as he suddenly burst into a fit of temper. "What does 'ours' mean? Every-body is ours, or should be. It is only human beings who invent such nonsense as 'ours' and 'theirs.' It is true that there are different breeds, according to dif-ferent natural habits and qualities, but in the matter of life and death all are alike."

"Papa," my sister, who was less timid than I in speaking to our father, interrupted, "why didn't the geese and the ducks look out for themselves? Why is it that we must look after them all?"

"They do look out for themselves and they post their sentinels as we do, but they don't know how to do it properly. They have much less of this stuff here than we cranes," and Papa tapped my sister's head lightly with his beak.

"And if God gave us better understanding of things and better gifts, we should use them for the benefit of our weaker and lesser brothers, as well as for our own. It is only thus that we can thank God, who gave us these superior talents. Do you understand?"

"We understand," we both answered, together.

"Well," said Mama, "I believe you've scolded them enough. The children are tired from their first night duty and sufficiently punished by what they have seen. Let them sleep now for an hour or so, instead of making them listen to sermons."

"It serves them right," smiled Papa, and he went to see Longnose and to inquire after the sick Trifler, who was hiding himself somewhere in the thicket.

Everything was very quiet up to noon and we had an excellent rest. Then Mother woke us and told us it had been decided to cut short our respite. The effect of the bloody incident was too strong. Nobody felt like staying in that neighborhood and orders were given for a take-off in the afternoon.

We were to fly along the Dnieper down to the city of Kiev, then to turn westward in the direction of the mouth of the Danube.

CHAPTER XI

OVELY is the Dnieper in still weather when its waters glide freely and smoothly through forest and mountain . . ." But it is not my own stuff. I'm sure I am borrowing it from one of the classics. Which one? Do you know?

But there is no doubt that the Dnieper is wonderful. And it is hard to say which of its two banks is lovelier—the right, with its steep, rocky slopes falling into the deep blue waters, or the low left bank stretching like a vast luxuriant carpet that melts away into blue distances. Scattered here and there were the picturesque southern villages, with their whitewashed cottages sunk in the green of their gardens, with their churches and the proud mansions of their country squires and their crowded harbors seething with life. And up and down the river, rafts, barges, ships, and steamers of all kinds dragged heavily or glided swiftly. White gulls fluttered in the air, now touching the surface of the water with their wings, now diving and coming up again in a silvery sparkle—a fish in their beaks.

There was much animation on the yellow sun-lit sandbanks. Here fishermen were spreading their nets, there they were covering the bottom of a big-bellied barge with pitch or fastening together the long logs of rafts. Farther along the beach a drove of cows, taken to be watered, rested in the shadow of looming rocks. Still farther away a beautiful bright spot was made by a group of women and children who had come down for a swim in the river.

Oxen with high horns were silently enjoying their bath in the water, away from annoying gadflies.

Thousands of streams and rivulets rushed along through the ravines and poured into the wide

Dnieper. The noisy well-wheels turned incessantly and church bells sounded from afar. That sound came from the direction where the dim outlines of towering monasteries and the churches of a large city rose out of the mist.

"That is Kiev," Longnose announced. "Centuries upon centuries it has stood there. Our fathers and forefathers used to pass over it in their flights south. Thousands of generations of cranes have flown over it, and it was always from this point that they turned southwest, heading for the mouth of the Danube."

"An ancient city," confirmed Papa.

"A delightful city!" my sister exclaimed. "But if this Dnieper were to flow through that other city— remember the one with ever so many churches and the house with a golden roof?—and the river that flows there were here, it would be——"

"And if you had a peacock's tail," the Trifler laughingly interrupted her, "and reindeer horns on your head, goodness knows what you would be. But you certainly would no longer be the pretty graceful cranny that you are."

My sister was about to grow angry, but the end

of the last sentence pleased her and the little minx smiled.

"Always trying to be funny!"

Meantime we were nearing the magnificent city. Situated on the high, rocky bank of the Dnieper, Kiev was built on the tiers of terraces that sloped down to the river, and was reflected in the waters as in a mirror. We were struck by its majestic beauty. Mountain tops crowned by ancient monasteries and churches with their thousands of gold and colored domes and exquisitely carved crosses made a lovely picture against the bright blue sky. The luxuriant verdure of the gardens hung down the slopes, clung to the edges of the cliffs, expanded into whole parks and squares, and made a beautiful setting for the long, crowded avenues.

Two bridges suspended over the Dnieper linked the city with the lowlands. Railroad trains passed over one with a clattering roar; over the other moved all sorts of vehicles and endless strings of pedestrians with bark knapsacks on their backs.

These were pilgrims from the four corners of our land going to kneel before the ancient shrines and the sacred relics of Kiev. The procession of pilgrims stretched as far as the high, square-notched stone walls of the monasteries on the outskirts of the city. Groups of them were resting in the shadow of the great walls while others moved to and fro and crowded through the dark arched gateways.

The long black clothes and high black cowls of some were conspicuous among the glaring colors of the pilgrim throng. They moved slowly and soberly and seemed to command unusual respect from the crowd.

Beyond the city we saw a military camp with its orderly squares of white tents. Firearms glittered and shots could be heard coming from that direction. We were naturally frightened at first, but as soon as we discovered that they were not meant for us we paid no further attention to them, and as we flew over the camp we trumpeted in response to their signal horns.

Soon the gray mist and clouds of dust rising from the city began to veil the lovely panorama. The city clamor grew fainter, then ceased altogether. The blue ribbon of the Dnieper went off to our left and below us the endless plains and straight highways stretched once again.

We must have been flying very high. We saw the

luminous circle of the sun, still above the horizon, but a dense curtain of twilight below was already quenching the last gleams of the church crosses and the golden glow of the Dnieper.

Again we descended to the stubble land. The place was open, easy to guard and therefore absolutely safe.

We fell asleep immediately and so soundly that when I opened my eyes half the sky was already lit by the dawn while the last stars were shining feebly, sinking in the flush of the dawning day.

"This is the sixth day of our trail," Longnose announced. "That is what a sturdy young stock will do. How different from last year! We certainly have done marvelously well!"

"Last year we didn't reach here until the end of the ninth day of travel," Papa said.

"And not without loss of our young birds at that," Mother added with a sigh.

"If you fly properly," said Uncle Kloo-Kloo, one of our old cranes, "you can travel very successfully. One thing strikes me as funny—that we don't see the other cranes here, those from the Ural Mountains. It is certainly time for them to be here. Shall we wait for them?"

"It may be that they went on ahead of us. We'd better find out," said Papa.

"By all means. Those bustards roaming about over there belong here. They ought to know."

"Let us see."

Several large heavy birds were wandering about a short distance away. Some of them raised their heads and gazed in our direction with evident curiosity. Flocks of partridges bustled about in the stubble and tiny comely quails flitted to and fro.

Sharp short whistles sounded from time to time, and we caught sight of some small, speckled animals that stood up on their hind legs, whistled, and hid themselves in their burrows again, then repeated the performance.

"Look at the number of marmots here," Uncle Kloo-Kloo said. "The grain must have suffered greatly from them."

Papa, accompanied by two young cranes, flew to the bustards for information about the Uralian cranes. We were walking peacefully along, discussing hundreds of different things, when a big gray animal appeared from a hollow and trotted through the fields, looking furtively from side to side. We knew him by his erect ears, his wicked bloodshot eyes, and his peculiar teeth. It was a wolf. He must have been very tired; his tongue hung limp from one side of his

SCATTERED HERE AND THERE WERE THE PIC-
TURESQUE SOUTHERN VILLAGES

mouth and the white foam was pouring out. His tail drooped, almost touching the ground.

To scamper away, was our first thought. But we saw instantly that it wasn't worth while. The wolf could think of nothing but his own safety. He turned his head and looked back in hatred and fear. Then he paused and dropped to the ground, hiding himself in the tall grass that grew along the hedge. Breathing heavily, he licked his hind leg.

Now we perceived far off some specks moving in our direction. These were riders approaching us at long strides; each of them held two pair of dogs on leash and some metal object slung on his back.

"Guns?" we thought.

"Those are bugles." Longnose quieted us, as if guessing our silent uneasiness. "We don't have to be afraid of them. But that rascal over there won't get away with a whole skin."

"I hope they don't notice him," I said, pitying the tracked animal.

"But they have already. See! They're turning to the right, cutting off his way of retreat."

It was clear now that the wolf was lost. Two more riders with dogs appeared, trotting ahead. The wolf saw them and started away. The riders unleashed the dogs and cantered after the wolf.

We kept on the alert, yet stayed where we were for we wanted to know how it would all end.

The wolf ran along the hedge and the cloud of dust rising above the grass betrayed his progress; his pursuers rushed across.

The first pair of dogs attacked him; then one of them jumped away, howling with pain. The wolf broke away and was now far ahead of them.

"Thank God! He will get away!" my sister exclaimed.

But then we thought of the poor cow and her calf, and we could not help feeling that their death was now about to be justly avenged.

The wolf was decidedly in a bad fix; one of the dogs, the largest of them all, flashed through the fields. The poor marauder hugged the ground, his teeth chattering, then, mustering all his strength, leaped up, and galloped through the field. A beautiful, fleet black dog dashed at him and clung to his ear. Another hit him with all his might in the flank. All three of them then rolled on the ground. Other dogs rushed in. Finally one of the riders came to the scene and, jumping down, pulled out his hunting knife. A raucous yelp sounded and died away.

Then other hunters picked the dead wolf up and they all went away.

Papa came back from his visit to the bustards and said that they had not seen any other parties of cranes so far, but had heard rumors that they were due any day, as the wild pigeons, who had passed that way, had seen them three days before.

"So that's how the matter stands," Papa said. "And how is everything here?"

"We saw a wolf hunted down. See them going away?"

"Fine!"

"How about this case, Grandpa? Was it banditry or industry?" My sister asked saucily.

"You little rascal," Grandfather Longnose smiled. "This—well—it was industry, if you like, or rather a punishment for robbery, burglary, and throat cutting, a punishment severe but just."

"How terrible!"

"It is, to those who aren't used to such things," the Trifler said scornfully. "When I was in Egypt I saw people killing other people. Those who killed were white people dressed from top to toe, those who were killed were naked black people. Then, in another place I saw naked black people killing the white, dressed people. That was a frightful sight, I must say."

"But why did they kill each other?" we wondered.

"There must have been a reason, but I never bothered finding it out."

"Stop your murder stories, or the children won't sleep," said Mamma. "Bloodshed is a great sin before God and, thank heaven, it is never committed by us cranes."

"Yes, but the storks practise it," the Trifler began. "I saw myself——"

"They must have learned it from the people. They get along so wonderfully together," said Mamma sharply.

"The bustards told me that they had a casualty yesterday evening—the hunters shot four of their flock," Papa began. "And it is curious how it happened. Live and learn is right. Two carts, loaded with straw, turned from the road toward them. The bustards never worried and as the cartloads passed near, they gaped like fools. As the carts encircled the camp, a hunter jumped out and fired. The bustards rushed away only to come upon other hunters who had hidden themselves in the tall grass. That's how they lost four of their friends. 'Now we shall certainly be more careful,' they said."

"They are careful all right," Longnose said, "but very absentminded and forgetful."

"I once saved a whole flock of them," the Trifler interjected. "The circumstances were exactly the same as you have just described them to us. But I saw the whole thing and I shouted to the bustards: 'Look out! Where are you going? Here!' Thank goodness, they had enough sense to listen to me."

"You certainly have a story up your sleeve for every occasion," Longnose laughed. "Well, well, even if it never happened, it might have and you would undoubtedly have acted gallantly."

"There is nothing incredible about it"—the Trifler sounded slightly offended—"and I really cannot understand why it should be doubted. Now take, for instance, another case. Believe it or not, but it did happen. Once I stole close to a hunter who was sound asleep. I presume he was drunk, as an empty vodka barrel lay near him. I saw a gun, and it was loaded.

'That's fine,' I thought, and snatching the gun I rose in the air. It must have been too heavy for me, or perhaps I was holding it the wrong way, but I began trying to change its position to a more comfortable one and it's possible that I pulled the trigger. The gun fired itself. That, of course, wouldn't have been worth mentioning, but imagine! . . . A large eagle was flying by, carrying a partridge in his claws. The bullet went straight into his head. The eagle screamed, turned over in the air, and struck the ground with such force that all his feathers fell out. I went right down after him. To my surprise the partridge was alive! She stretched me her dainty claw and said: 'Thank you, my noble deliverer! Thank you! You have saved the mother of a hundred and twenty-seven children!' And really, I saw a whole flock of them running out of the grass. I counted them—there were exactly a hundred and twenty-seven and they all squeaked, 'Thank you! Thank you!' I was deeply moved and tears stood in my eyes as I said to them: 'I wish you happiness, my children; as for me, I have only done my duty!' "

"Isn't he a good sport!" Papa roared. "One certainly never gets bored listening to his stories!"

"Is it true?" And my sister looked imploringly into the eyes of the narrator.

"As if I ever lie! As if I am capable of——"

"Thank you." My sister scratched the Trifler's wing tenderly with her beak.

"Hm," said Mother, and she glanced meaningly at Father.

Papa also said, "Hm," twice, and added in an undertone but so that we could all hear him, "Nonsense!"

CHAPTER XII

HE pigeons were right. At about dawn, before we had left our shelter, we heard a familiar hissing sound and the noise of powerful wings —and a great flock of cranes came down at a little distance from us.

Several cranes, evidently the leaders, immediately stepped forth. Those of our band who went to meet them were Longnose, Papa, and the Trifler, who wouldn't stay behind.

These cranes, as we had been told, were the combined forces from the Kama River and the Ural

Mountains who had met at Moscow and continued their journey together. They were of exactly the same breed as we, and our senior cranes found old acquaintances and friends among them—especially our grandsire Longnose. One of the newcomers, a crane of great age, even kissed our leader and they began dancing, wing to wing, in honor of their reunion. Though both of them danced exquisitely, our Longnose was the more graceful. Then Longnose introduced his friend, "the Wise Wing Flap," to my father and mother.

"I have the honor and pleasure to be an ancient friend of the most Wise Longnose," and the leader of the Kamo-Uralian cranes saluted courteously.

"Yes, old man," our grandsire said, "we have passed through many a sorrow and many a joy together in this life!"

"We certainly have," sighed the other. "What a lovely young stock you have this year! So well fattened and strong! And they seem to show not the slightest fatigue from the journey. But, of course, with such a leader as you, they have nothing to worry about!"

"But yours—they are in excellent shape too! Your talents for leadership are unsurpassed!"

"Come, come! What about yourself? You are too modest!"

"No, I mean it. Did you suffer any loss?"

"Yes, we did. On our third stretch two of the youngsters ate something wrong and died. Then one three-year old crane was shot."

"Too bad! How was that?"

"Shot by a long-range gun. And we were never able to find out where the shot came from. People provide themselves with such guns nowadays that they upset all our calculations."

Following the lead of our elders, we young birds also became acquainted and soon friendly. Animated chatter was audible all over the giant crane camp.

As the newcomers had flown the whole preceding night, they needed a full day's rest. And as we were to continue the journey together, we also had to stay.

It was a very happy day. The people didn't annoy us nor, in fact, did anyone else. True, several eagles and vultures circled about in the air over our heads but, seeing our numbers, they never dared come down.

Our Trifler lingered among the newcomers all day. He was undoubtedly telling them his stories. My sister was somehow annoyed by this. But towards evening our tale teller returned—and stayed with us till sunset. He danced in our circle and even volunteered to stand sentinel when it was the turn of my triangle. As this did not interfere with the general schedule, he was allowed to do as he pleased.

At dawn, filled with vigor by the prolonged rest, we started. It was an interesting and imposing sight. Even the people traveling along the state road stopped their carriages and, shading their eyes from the sun's rays, watched as triangle after triangle detached itself from the yellowish-gray fields, rose smoothly and symmetrically into the air, and took its place in the gigantic wedge extending over half the firmament.

The choir of our trumpets sounded sharply in the fresh morning air, and Papa the Clarion's blast was louder than anyone else's.

The bustards were preparing to leave too and watched our take-off with secret envy. Poor things!

That day we saw a forest fire. My! What a distressing sight that was!

The fire had started in a wide clearing and spread

creeping along the ground. Occasionally an old tree, licked by the flames, would blaze to its very top, a beautiful column of fire, its branches writhing as it burned. The ominous sound of crashing trees and roaring flames echoed far and wide. Sparks and firebrands were blown about by a strong wind and the columns of black resinous smoke poisoned the thickening air.

How many poor little animals and tiny birds, suffocated by the smoke, unable to fly, fell into the all-devouring blaze!

There, on the edge of the forest, a small tree had caught fire. Screams and cries for help could be heard coming from that direction. Somewhere in the dense smoke the alarm bell was ringing unceasingly. Hundreds of people hurried about, digging ditches to cut the fire off from the approach to their village. At the same time they were hastily removing their belongings from the cottages and loading them on wagons.

We were compelled to detour from our route through fear of suffocation. The heavy odor of the smoke haunted us till nightfall, and we suffered from throat irritation all the following day. The forest regions were left far behind. The scenery changed to an endless vista of steppes, but even here the bitter bluish mist hung over everything.

Sparsely populated and burnt by the hot sun, the steppes were now lifeless and dreary. They rolled smoothly along, cut only occasionally by ravines. The whitewashed huts of the Little Russians, their yellow cornstalks, and the highways were all that relieved the monotony of the landscape.

They had funny-looking wells in this region and, pointing to them, the Trifler said to us: "They look every inch like ourselves! Don't they?"

"How do you mean?"

"Well, the joke is that they call them 'cranes' in these provinces. Ha, ha, ha," the Trifler laughed. "But there is certainly no resemblance whatever—a pitiful parody."

I must say, I didn't agree with the Trifler. When such a well is in action it certainly does look like a bird pecking the water with its beak. I don't see any reason for calling them "cranes," but they most certainly do suggest storks and possibly herons.

Large flocks of bleating sheep crowded about the

wells with their shepherds in tattered clothes, swearing loudly.

Then we saw wide fields of melons and watermelons. Their dry thin stalks crept intertwined along the ground, and heavy balls, dark green, yellow, and almost white, lay glistening in the sun, "to stick the beak into which was rather pleasant," as Papa said.

"In due time we shall try them," Longnose promised us. "Very likely it will be during our next rest."

And our leader kept his word. We tried them. Sweet and tender as they were, we found both these fruits more suitable for quenching the thirst than for nourishment, though the melons were somewhat more solid.

We had passed many cities and towns, many villages and hamlets, had seen some chains of mountains, blue in the distance, when, on our third day's journey from Kiev, Papa told us to take a good look at what was lying before us.

Before us lay a limitless water basin flowing into an immense, triangular piece of marshy ground, thick with reeds and intersected by numberless streams of water, narrow and wide.

114

"This is the mouth of the Danube," Longnose told us, "a wonderful country for waders like us and for birds generally who have no aversion to water."

"And that, over there?" I asked, pointing to a dark-blue streak on the horizon from which came a peculiar sound, a sort of noise, but nothing like the noise of a large city, nor the howling of a distant gale, nor anything familiar.

"That is the Black Sea."

"Oh—oh—oh!" All the young birds exclaimed.

And we all looked reverently and not altogether without awe in the direction of the distant blue streak. The sea—a limitless expanse of water which you cannot cross if you are not sure that your wings are strong enough. Should they fail for a moment— down you go into the depths. And drowning is not the only misfortune that awaits you in the sea—some big fish may snap you up alive, which Mother told us often happens. We cranes never could hope to cross the sea. When traveling we keep as near the shore as we can.

But, oh, what a wonderful place the mouth of the Danube is! What a multitude of all sorts of migratory birds! The great flocks that we had seen on the

Dnieper shallows seemed now a mere trifle. Only here, seeing these huge gatherings, could we understand fully the advantages of flying in great crowds. One simply feels lost among these enormous masses.

Here for the first time in our lives we met the pelicans. They were magnificent large birds, pinkish white in color, with huge beaks and deep pouches on their lower jaws. They were busy fishing, and as there were plenty of fish the pelicans kept on swallowing them and storing some away in their pouches, which were so loaded with fish that they hung down heavily. These birds, who are known for their rather surly dispositions, were not easily drawn into conversation. But the lovely swans chatted gayly with us. They swam in the deep waters, raising their superb feathers in the form of a sail and flapping their wings.

A few dozen of herons were about to start a foolish fight for the place we had taken. But, seeing our superior forces, they retreated.

We had taken possession of an entire island where we could stay till dusk. The place was very attractive, but there was absolutely no food except fish, for which we cranes do not care. Later we intended feeding on the cornfields that were near the village and, to make matters worse, were fenced in by wattling. With this in view, our elders had divided the whole caravan into small parties which were to take turns at the cornfields, to prevent the clamor and attention that the great flocks always excite.

On the whole it must be said that, despite the luxuriant vegetation, it was growing more and more difficult to provide food.

"Please take note of this as a general rule," said Papa, "the more people have, the stingier they grow and the more jealous they guard their possessions. And they are right in a way. Remember, we are out of our land of plenty. The time of abundant and palatable meals is over. Lent will last till the mouth of the Nile, where again we shall find food in plenty."

"Is the Nile near already?" my sister asked. She had caught the word "Nile" and was on tiptoe. We had all heard so much about that fabulous river that the very mention of its name gave us a thrill.

"No, not very near," Papa answered. "But in view of the scarcity of food we shall have to fly faster, and in three or four days we shall see the Nile, dead sand deserts, pyramids, obelisks, sphinxes, and other remarkable things of which I think it better to say nothing so that your impressions may be keener and more vivid."

When it grew dark our first party flew to sup in the cornfields and soon returned safely. Our turn came sixth.

Though it was with some apprehension that we saw the bright lights in the houses near by and heard the loud talking of the people, who for some reason did not sleep, we were too hungry to pay much attention to them and we hastily filled our crops by pecking at the heavy, ripe ears and shelling the beautiful, mealy kernels with our beaks.

"This is nice, but the peas taste so much better!" my sweet-toothed sister said.

"This isn't bad either," I decided.

But our Trifler, who for my sister's sweet sake had promised unconditional obedience and obtained Papa's permission to go with our party, was now trying to break away the whole ear.

"Don't be so greedy," whispered one of our cranes to him.

"It is not for myself," and the Trifler winked as he finally managed to tear the ear away.

We spoke in whispers, so as not to be heard by

the people. But we couldn't fool the dogs. They would rush at us every once in a while, barking fiercely, so that we had to get up and fly away for a time.

As soon as we heard the wing flaps of the approaching seventh party we immediately made way for them and, preserving our usual military order, returned to our island. We had learned that discipline and order were the best guarantees of success, especially when we were away from home and flying in such great numbers.

The night was dark and starry. The milky way, cutting the sky in two, stood out with such precision and sharpness as never before. The heavy roar of the sea reached our ears; we could even hear the splashing and the dull boom of the waves against the sandy shore.

CHAPTER XIII

 O THERE it was at last—
the sea! A shoreless, dark-
blue, rolling expanse melted
away into the horizon, and
grumbled as if resenting our
bold threat to fly over its
depths.

Below fluttered seagulls,
large and small, clearing the foamy white crests of the
waves, diving and filling the air with their shrieks.

Shiny black dolphins played and leaped, chasing
the fish. The salty air was cool. Loose rugged clouds,
heralds of a strong wind, moved swiftly in the sky.
Something dark and ominous was approaching from

the east, threatening to develop into a real storm at about noon.

To our right was a narrow shore line; farther off one could discern the dots of beacon lights and the outlines of a fortress. The mouth of the Danube was now left far behind.

We were cutting the distance considerably by flying over the sea instead of following the course of the coast, and soon we perceived through the clouds to our right the bluish ridges of some high mountains.

"These are the Balkan Mountains," the old-timers told us. And there, it seemed, was a city in the midst of the sea. White needles from the lighthouse towers flashed all over the place. A long stone wall built far into the sea sheltered a veritable forest of masts and sails. The sea below us roared and the waves piled higher and higher, striding wrathfully forward and crushing one another. And there, beyond the long wall, the surface was perfectly smooth and calm. The ships standing there hardly rocked and thousands of rowboats, filled with boxes, barrels, and people in white turbans and red fezzes, glided about.

"This is Varna," Longnose said to us. "As soon as

we pass it we shall turn toward the shore, where there is a good resting place for us."

That was welcome news! It was just what we needed. This last stretch had seemed to us all much more of a strain than any preceding it. The Trifler attributed this to the wind that hindered our progress. And indeed it was very noticeable—blowing from the side and pushing us much farther to the right than our course demanded. If we had encountered such a wind at the beginning of our journey we would certainly have been unable to withstand it. But now that our wings had developed their full strength, we were equal to the test. Besides, we ran no real risks as the shore was not far away.

When we had passed Varna our whole army was arranged into a fanlike wedge and directed shoreward. These orders were given because of the density of the population in this country where it was difficult to find a camp for such a troop as ours. Then, again, there were considerations of safety. The night with its secure darkness, and therefore our supper, was still far off, and we went down only to rest our tired, wind-beaten wings.

Our party descended to a barren mountain slope

near a railway track. A train puffed along heavily and noisily. A file of squeaky two-wheeled wagons, drawn by buffaloes, crawled up the slope. Near us grazed a small herd of goats under the care of a pretty shepherdess with a wreath of red flowers on her curly black hair; she rode on a little gray donkey who cropped prickly grass as he moved along.

I won't say that we were hungry, but we were beginning to feel that we wouldn't mind having a bite. Papa was already planning to despatch the scouts to find some pasture land or gardens.

"This is for you, my pretty Miss," and the Trifler placed a fine ear of corn at my sister's feet.

He had carried it all the way from the mouth of the Danube.

My sister seemed abashed and looked questioningly at Mamma. The latter smiled approvingly and said to Papa, "That's fine! It looks as if our Trifler would make a good husband!"

"Yes, if he stops playing the fool," Papa agreed.

My sister pretended to be unconcerned and shelled the ear gracefully with her beak so that we could all share in the delicacy.

123

"You must have some, too," she said to the Trifler, "or I will not touch it either."

"Certainly," and the Trifler leaped in and picked out the smallest and driest of all the kernels.

All this was very stirring and I couldn't forgive myself for not having done likewise. Why had I eaten so much myself, without ever thinking of anybody else? Mother would have appreciated it so much, or Papa.

But, to tell the truth, I was feeling particularly angry with myself because, in addition to my parents, there was someone else I would have liked to treat. Yes, I was thinking of a young cranny whose appearance had attracted me the very first day we had met. All I knew about her was that she belonged to the Uralian triangles, but where she was now I had no idea. I lived in the hope that as soon as we reached the Delta of the Nile we should all camp together again and then—and then—— Oh, then I should certainly be as smart as that prig of a Trifler, and I too would find a way of making myself agreeable and even attractive.

And I was transported by visions of that wonderful moment of our future meeting, and absentmindedly I began to gulp the corn kernels in such haste that my sister tapped me on the side and said reproachfully. "Think of the others, you little glutton!"

"Let the boy have all the corn he wants," the Trifler interfered in my behalf. "Youngsters of his age always have a good appetite."

His condescending remark infuriated me more than that of my sister and I felt like fighting my advocate.

Our scouts came back and reported that they had found a vineyard, but the people were working there constantly, so there was no way of approaching it. But the local sparrows had told them that about two miles from our camp there were hemp fields and Bulgarian vegetable gardens with beans and lentils, and that though the village was very close to the gardens, it was so situated that we might hope to escape unnoticed in the darkness.

We had soon reached the hemp fields and could see from there the thatched roofs of the Bulgarian cottages and the white tower of a minaret. We were very unpleasantly affected by the sight of a great number of shaggy storks' nests. They were everywhere—on every roof. The minaret held a whole cluster of them, and they were visible on all the higher crosses of the cemetery near by and on all the cypresses growing around the cemetery. And we could see the storks themselves flying over the roofs reddened by the rays of the setting sun.

We weren't sure whether they really failed to notice us, or only pretended to, but we had no difficulty in entrenching ourselves in the hemp fields and moving toward the bean beds.

So completely different from our northland, there is no twilight in these countries. The minute the sun sets, impenetrable darkness falls and we were eagerly awaiting that moment.

We groped for the bean beds and began to eat, calling to each other in low voices so as to keep together. Following the example of the Trifler, I pulled out a whole bunch of bean plants and twisted them around my neck.

"Enough," sounded the signal, and we started back to the hemp fields. The darkness was such that we decided to wait there until daylight rather than fly at random to our camp.

At daybreak we were awakened by the angry

shrieks of the storks and our own war signals. Somewhere near the village a great disturbance was raging.

The shrieks and cries grew louder and louder, and we heard the sound of clashing wings and the moans of the wounded.

We promptly drew ourselves up in battle array and rushed to the rescue of our own.

"One for all!" Papa, the Clarion, shouted, "and all for one!"

We reached the scene, arriving in the nick of time. A whole army of storks had fallen unexpectedly on one of our Uralian triangles. The odds were five to one. But the Uralians fought gallantly, though several cranes had been wounded and had fallen helpless into the grass.

We rushed upon the enemy, sounded our battle cry, and instantly threw them into confusion. Under my very eyes the Trifler knocked a stork down and went in pursuit of another. Papa, the Clarion, was striking them left and right. But the forces of the storks still far outnumbered ours and new flocks were drawing in from every side to help them. But just when we were beginning to lose ground, we heard again the glad sound of our trumpets. More of our triangles were rushing to our aid, and at the head of them all was the Wise Wing Flap. Our new reinforcements instantly overthrew the entire stork army so that they were compelled to retreat from the battleground. They began mustering their strength near the cemetery, preparing for a new attack.

"Retreat!" sounded the order of the Wing Flap.

"Why? How can we?" the indignant murmuring of the young birds was heard.

"Retreat without arguing when you are ordered!" thundered Papa, the Clarion. "Stop, youngsters! Back! The commander knows what he is about! They can see it better from above!"

And indeed, we heard voices and, raising our heads, saw our grandsire Longnose with two triangles formed into one. They were making warning signs to us circling about with a continuous, harsh, guttural cry of alarm. We began our retreat and soon saw that people with long guns were running to the scene of battle. Several thin puffs of smoke burst from below. Several bullets hissed by—but fortunately without causing us any harm.

Though the storks were the friends of man, as they

boastfully asserted, the sound of the shots had frightened them no less than us and they dispersed, hiding themselves somewhere, without any pretense of pursuit.

As soon as we were once more in safety, an inquiry was started as to the circumstances leading to the fight. It appeared that the storks had begun it. They pretended to object to our pillaging the people's fields. In reality, they were simply looking for some excuse to insult our cranes, who wouldn't stand for it. The fight began and ended in bloodshed. If help had not come in time it might have resulted in the destruction of an entire triangle. As it was now, we had lost four of our cranes and had about ten wounded. And all this for what?

"For the beans," somebody said.

"No, not exactly for the beans. The storks don't eat them. Why should they care if we ravage the whole field? But they were defending the interests of man and, after all, they were right," Uncle Kloo-Kloo decided.

"Beans and other vegetables are made by God for our use. It is true that these beans were planted by the people and were their private property. But it wasn't our fault that there were no others—wild beans, for example—in this neighborhood. We had to eat. And if the people were less unfriendly to us cranes, we in our turn would certainly render them some service, such as—such as, for example——"

Here Papa faltered in his thought, unable to find a suitable example. Longnose came to his aid.

"Our friend, the Clarion, has just told us a great truth. We had to eat. And that's all there is to it."

We all agreed to that and decided that from that viewpoint we cranes were perfectly right.

"It always happens so with the people when, after a fierce conflict, they begin to talk and try to find justification for their actions," said the Wise Wing Flap. "It transpires that both sides were right. Once I witnessed a terrible, bloody battle that took place in this very land. Armies of people in blue clothes and red fezzes marched against people in gray clothes and white caps. Both sides proclaimed the war 'for the true God,' and, calling on His name, began to fight. And what a fight it was! It was mutual wholesale destruction. And both sides were right and so sincerely believed in their righteousness that for the sake of it they gladly sacrificed their lives. And those who survived undoubtedly believed in it up to this day and will bequeath the belief to their children and grandchildren. What was it then, for which they fought? Was it really for the true God? No, but they won't know that till later. I believe that the souls of the fallen heroes on both sides will meet beyond and only there discover the final truth. But here, on this earth, nobody will ever understand anything that is going on. But what is this?" And the old philosopher pointed to my side. "Is he a hero distinguished in this morning's action, or what? What are these decorations?"

General attention was now focused on me and I felt so embarrassed that I didn't know what to do. They all looked at the bean plants twisted around my neck. Then the Trifler came to me and said, as he tapped me affectionately with his beak: "That's fine. Always follow good examples and you will be all right. These beans are much easier to carry than the ears of corn."

The sun had risen and it was time for us to start. The people were awakening. Their chimneys were already smoking; they were up again at their daily activities.

Mourning our losses and speaking kind words in memory of our fallen cranes, we broke up into triangles and departed.

But before we went I had the satisfaction of finding and offering the beans to the charming Uralian cranny who reigned in my thoughts.

CHAPTER XIV

E CONTINUED to fly over the sea. But this time we kept nearer the coast, densely packed with cities, villages, and gardens. Another coast, high and steep, was dimly seen in the distance ahead of us. Between these two coasts lay a narrow waterway and on it something white and golden glittered faintly in the sunlight.

The fog over the sea, pierced by the sun's rays, began to melt away and a magnificent spectacle now lay before us. The narrow waterway widened and we

133

saw the entrance to a fortified strait. The heavy outlines of gloomy fortress walls and huge cannon lurking in the embrasures contrasted sharply with the
exquisite castles and villas scattered along the beautiful banks of the strait, with the bright foliage of
the gardens and the lovely garlands of flowers hanging over the balustrades and fences. Scores of
steamers and other ships moved along the strait and
stood in picturesque groups at the piers. There were
so many of them that it seemed as if the vessels from
all the seas came here, and this was very likely the
case. Here too were heavy, formidable warships,
guarding the entrance to this enchanting place.
Farther away lay the city; such lovely minarets and
such stately cupolas I had never seen in my life. The
lively beat of the city traffic and the muffled sound
of human voices reached us from afar. But near the
warships all was still and desolate, as if the presence
of these iron-clad monsters frightened and drove
away all that was living and cheerful.

On the other bank of the strait were more shady
gardens, rows of slender cypresses, and cozy cottages
with latticed balconies, entwined by trailing flowers
and ivy.

"TSARIGRAD!" PAPA ANNOUNCED, "OR, AS
OTHERS CALL IT, CONSTANTINOPLE."

It seemed that the colonies on both banks of the strait lived a common life and formed one community.

"Tsarigrad!" Papa announced, "or, as others call it, Constantinople. And this," as he pointed to our left, "is Scutari."

Goodness knows what we would have given for permission to descend and take a good look at all those wonders, but in obedience to our high command we flew farther and farther, leaving far behind that bewitching city with its curious street life.

Now we were flying over another sea—the Sea of Marmora. The lovely blue of its waters bears no resemblance to that stone. But there were many small islands scattered through the sea containing marble quarries, so that must account for its name. We were crossing the Sea of Marmora from the northwest to the southeast, and though we began to feel considerable fatigue, there was no place where we could go down and rest. Fortunately, a favorable breeze, soft and scented, helped our progress to a great measure. Toward evening we had another picturesque Asiatic city—Brusa. The district was mountainous and through the light clouds before us a mighty peak loomed. As we passed over Brusa, the plaintive sounds of a muezzin calling the faithful to prayer reached our ears. We steered toward the great peak and came down over an open, barren, stony valley at its foot. We didn't expect to find much to eat there, but at least we could rest peacefully. There were no human dwellings in sight but a few shepherd huts were huddled near a brook under an old many-branched sycamore.

The mountain at whose foot we were encamped was called Keshish-Dag. At about an hour's flight from us two fairly large lakes glimmered through the night mist. But the haunts surrounding them were already occupied by birds of other breeds and, fearing a new clash, we decided to stay where we were and content ourselves with a few scrubby bushes of wild raspberries growing here and there out of the rocky crevices.

It was the period of the new moon and the thin sickle appeared timidly in the dark sky for a short time.

A long autumn night, or what we would have called in the north summer night, passed undisturbed.

As I slumbered I thought of my Uralian cranny. "Where is she now? What is she doing? Has she enough to eat? Does she sleep quietly?" I found comfort in thinking that she was under the secure protection of the Wise Wing Flap himself, who was the leader of her triangle. Where were they now?

"I hope our friends are camping in some better place," the Trifler said to me, as if reading my thoughts. "They are flying along the coast, they must have passed Mytilene by now."

"Where is that?"

"That is an island near the coast. I was there once. It is known for its wonderful bay that is cut deep into the island, and no matter how rough the sea is it's always quiet in that bay. It used to be a favorite retreat for pirates."

"Merciful heavens! And to think that she is there!" I shrieked in terror.

"Who is 'she'?"

I felt altogether lost.

The Trifler laughed.

"Don't be foolish. No pirates bother with the cranes. But the young lady in question is certainly lovable. Her name is Blackneck. I met her father and mother yesterday."

So! The Trifler already knew her name and her family! Why did I dawdle and dally! Why was he so quick and full of energy, while I—— Why, I hardly deserved the name of a crane. I was as sluggish as an owl! I was so angry with myself and felt so provoked that ordinarily I would certainly have said something very harsh. But the Trifler sounded so sincere that I checked my temper and only repeated in a melancholy voice: "Blackneck!"

"Yes, Blackneck. She certainly doesn't stand comparison with your sister, but she is a very fine girl and I congratulate you."

"When shall we see them?" I asked longingly, beginning to credit the Trifler with knowing everything.

The latter seemed perplexed. He looked very grave and drew some incomprehensible signs and lines on the sand with his beak.

"There," he said at last. "You see, we are here now —that is our mountain. Here to the west lies the coast of the Sea of Marmora. Then it turns south and passing through here, at this point," and the

Trifler stuck his beak into the sand, "are the Dardan-elles. Then the coast turns to the east again and forms a great gulf. Facing this gulf lies the island of Mytilene, that I mentioned before. Then a whole string of small islands runs along the coast. These islands, tiny as they are, would do very well as rest-ing places and if we dared risk taking a short cut, thereby saving a great distance, and if the wind should be favorable, we could fly straight to the island of Cyprus. But what I think we shall have to do, is to cross the gulf of Alexandretta somewhat farther north and then glide down south toward Beirut, Damascus, Jerusalem, Port Said, Alexandria, and finally to the Delta of the great Nile!"

The Trifler grew so excited, showing off his learn-ing to me, that he completely forgot my question. I felt bewildered by all the geographical names he had mentioned, and couldn't make out the sketch he had drawn on the sand. So finally I ventured to stop him, repeating my question.

"Oh, yes," he said, "you are still at it. Well, I don't think we shall see them before we reach the Delta of the Nile. The country here is rather lean. To press in toward the mainland would be too hot and too far; the coastland is too crowded with people. But if we flew from here to Cyprus they might give us a good rest there."

"So we may meet them at Cyprus?"

"Very likely."

"Tell me, please, how is it that you know everything? Take me, for instance. I can give you no information about the places we have passed. I remember a few things that particularly struck me, but I should never be able to draw a map of them."

"Naturally, because it's your first trip. Everything is new to you and distracts your attention. With me it's another matter. I have traveled widely and am accustomed to making observations. Sometimes I even make notes of them. Wait till you've made as many journeys as I. You'll get there . . ."

"And how many flights have you made?"

The Trifler hesitated, but recovered immediately and mumbled something indefinite that might have been either "second" or "twenty-second."

"Second, is it?" I insisted, not without malice.

"What a wonderful night!" The Trifler sighed. "Your sister must sleep very soundly. And good-night to you, my friend. As for me, I can't sleep—I'll take a walk, I'll dream."

He tossed his head, shook his wings, looked toward the starry heaven, sighed, and disappeared in the darkness, stalking along the valley.

Strangely enough, my sister woke up too and stalked away. I felt sure it was none of my business and stuck my head under my wing. If only we could fly to Cyprus! And I dreamt that night about that wonderful island which I had never seen, but which my imagination pictured as the best place on this earth.

The next stretch proved rather uneventful. We flew over sparsely populated highlands. A few miserable hamlets, a few fields, and still fewer gardens were seen in the gorges. We were astonished at the number of people bearing weapons. Positively everybody here had a gun. And we saw several bloody encounters. Some people hiding among the rocks at the roadside lay in waiting for travelers whom they attacked, robbed, and killed. But more often they only threatened them, taking away their horses, cattle, and camels. A very unpleasant country indeed!

"No order here! In a word, Turkey!" Papa, the Clarion, said.

Reaching a beautiful lake lying in the rocky basin, we descended for a rest. Here we found several more of our parties, but alas! the triangle of the Wise Wing Flap was not among them.

"It looks as though we should fly to Cyprus," the Trifler whispered to me. "We're going straight toward the Gulf of Adalia, whereas otherwise we should have to keep to the east. Besides, the weather is wonderful for the flight over the sea."

We took off in the morning and passed over a mountain gorge through whose bed a narrow river wound, tumbling and foaming between the rocks. Then, against the deep blue background of the sea, we saw the neat outlines of a small white city.

This was the Gulf of Adalia. Following the coast line, we flew high, almost on a level with the summits of the ridges, and at the end of the day we came down to the arid shore of Cape Anamur, strewn with pebbles and mussels.

CHAPTER XV

HE Trifler was right. It had been decided to fly straight to Cyprus. The stretch to be covered was not very long, but there was always the danger of one of those sudden storms so frequent in these parts. Such storms, if combined with a strong adverse wind, or one blowing from the coast, presented grave perils. But all signs seemed to point to fair weather. Still there was disagreement among our elders as to the route we should take. Some of them held that the apparently favorable weather in these regions couldn't be de-

145

pended upon, and insisted on the flight along the coast of the Alexandretta Gulf. The majority, however, were for the Cyprus route and that decision was enthusiastically received by all the young birds, to say nothing of myself.

If only I could find out where the triangle of the Wise Wing Flap was! The garrulous seagulls swore to me that they had seen some cranes heading towards Cyprus the day before, but what cranes these had been they didn't know. To tell the truth, one could never learn anything from those hopeless fools of seagulls.

"I don't believe they were ours," the Trifler remarked. "They took a much longer route, so they cannot be ahead of us."

"Right," Papa confirmed.

We were comfortably quartered and our rest continued undisturbed. The shrill squeaking of the gulls and the eternal roar of the surf were the only sounds that broke the silence. To avoid the scorching sun we kept in the shadow cast by the high rocks on the coast. To amuse ourselves we would occasionally skip, standing on one spot, or run down to enjoy a shower bath in the spray of the waves that splashes against the rocks, or to look at the new mussels cast on the shore by each wave.

Towards evening other parties of cranes began to assemble. From them we learned that the Wing Flap, out of consideration for the rather weak young stock of his triangle, would not run the risk of a flight over the sea and was keeping along the coast farther north, steering towards Alexandretta.

The island of Cyprus had lost every attraction for me.

For a moment I even considered the vile thought of pretending fatigue. They might yet change the route for my sake! But my conscience revolted and my pride would not endure such humiliation, so with a heavy heart I submitted to my lot.

"Not before the Nile now," the Trifler smiled sympathetically.

That fellow positively guessed my every thought.

During the night two more triangles joined us. They had calculated that the majority would follow the way of the Wise Wing Flap.

But the weather continued fair and no signs of anything appeared to shake our decision.

We rested for another full day and part of the

night, till the narrow white streak appeared in the east.

The coast, still sunk in darkness, disappeared rapidly from sight. The summits of the ridge were already fringed with red, making a fantastic, jagged line against the somber background.

The Trifler asserted that he already saw the top of Kionistro—a huge mountain in the center of the island—but hard as we tried we could see nothing resembling it. The only thing we discovered was a blue cloud ahead of us that moved, then melted away in the azure of the new day. The outlines of the coast had now completely vanished from our sight and we seemed to be flying in an immense void. The sea below was smooth as a mirror—its shores melted into the sky. Above was the same boundless nothingness, as smooth, as quiet, and as blue as the sea. The sunshine was dazzling, and still more dazzling was its reflection in the smooth sea. And it seemed that the rays from above and the rays from below poured forth equally vigorous streams of life-giving warmth and love.

It was so natural, easy, and delightful to fly! Why did they doubt and fear this passage! Our trust in our leaders was so complete that the immensity of the void around us inspired no dread in us. We were not yet tired, we could have flown another whole day, but we were already near our goal. Before us, clear and distinct, as if rising from the waters, stood Kionistro, separated from the horizon line by a thin dark streak.

Then other lower peaks appeared—then the line of the coast with its white fringe of surf foam. Again we heard the roar and rumbling of the sea and the shrieks of the gulls and we saw the wild ivy hanging down over the rocks. No more than an hour's flight and we should be on solid ground.

But the sun had reached its zenith when, having passed the pretty city of Levkozia and its vineyards, we descended for a rest.

The success of this flight over the open sea, where no retreat was possible, redoubled our self-confidence, and now we thought without any anxiety of the future flight to Beirut, where the distance to be covered was twice as great.

We spent a quiet night. There was no indication of a change in the weather, and at dawn we started, more confident than ever in our lucky star and in the happy outcome of this passage.

At noon there was still no sign of firm land in sight. The smooth surface of the water below began to rock ominously, as if breathing heavily. But it was absolutely soundless. There was no splashing or anything to suggest roughness.

"Speed!" came the order from the front ranks.

"Speed!" The word was repeated along every line.

We were going at such speed now that the whistling of our wings echoed in the void.

The sea began to breathe more and more heavily. But there was no wind—complete calm reigned in the air. Below us a ship was standing motionless, all its sails spread; it creaked heavily as it rolled; now its stern, now its prow would sink deep into the water. Tiny half-naked people, wearing red fezzes, bustled about the rigging hurriedly taking in the sails. Occasional whistles could be heard and words of command.

"It looks rather bad to me," the Trifler said in a low voice, and quietly changed his post in the triangle, so that he was flying in front of me and directly behind my sister.

"Look to the left," he whispered again.

I saw something immense and dreadful covering almost half of the horizon; it moved toward us gaining in breadth, driving the heavy clouds ahead.

"Speed!" came again from the front.

But we were already flying at full speed and our wings, alas, were beginning to yield to fatigue. Foaming white snakes began creeping restlessly along the surface of the sea. The ship that we had encountered was now lost to sight. The first gust of wind, coming upon us suddenly, bent the straight lines of our triangles into curves.

But we preserved our order, working vigorously with our wings. Yet, strange to say, we seemed to be no longer moving forward but drifting, drifting irresistibly to the right. Then, together with a terrible, deafening, stupefying crash of thunder, came a jagged lightning flash, and it grew dark. Though the sun was still visible, it shed no rays; it looked like a dark red ball that gave no light.

"Keep together! Go with the wind!" sounded my papa's voice faintly.

But it was no longer possible to obey his command. Something heavy rushed by me, almost knocking me over. It was a crane torn away from the triangle and driven furiously along with the wind. He was revolving helplessly in the air, like a rag. For another moment he was visible, then he vanished in the darkness. . . . There went another victim. Then my sister began to wail plaintively. She was dropping down. She tossed her pretty head, kicking her feet desperately in the air. I saw the Trifler swoop down promptly, as if diving. Then the two birds, convulsively fighting the squall, dropped lower and lower until they were lost to sight.

Now I feel that I can stand it no longer. I can't! I can't! My ruin is near. I see nothing of what surrounds me—I am all alone. Am I flying up, or am I moving forward? I don't know. I don't feel anything. The black clouds press upon me. Below, some infernal monster roars. Suddenly I am drenched in cold water. My ears tingle. A huge green mountain with a foamy crest rises above me—below, a dark, yawning abyss. I start up, gathering all my strength. I cannot tell whether I fly up, but I am suddenly flung full force against something hard yet elastic, and I faint.

To my despair, when I came to my senses I saw

MY SISTER BEGAN TO WAIL PLAINTIVELY. SHE
WAS DROPPING DOWN

swarthy human faces about me and I felt the touch of a roughened hand on my back.

"In captivity," flashed through my mind, and immeditely the dreaded words, forever associated in my consciousness with captivity, "scissors" and "cord," occurred to me.

"Yes, he is alive," a voice said.

"Poor birds!" sounded another, sweet and melodious, the voice of a woman.

"Let him rest, he will be all right," said a third.

I was left alone and by and by I began to look about me.

The sky was starry, with a few tattered black clouds scurrying along. Above my head was a broken mast, its twisted cordage hanging, and people were puttering about it. There was another mast—this one in good order. A red light fell on a swelling sail; farther away there were other sails.

I must be on board a ship—on a deck strewn with the débris of rigging. The people were busy, the sound of an ax and of their voices could be heard. The light poured forth from below through a window with a broken pane; something was thrown overboard with a heavy splash. They pulled at a rope, which caught me and turned me over. I groaned with pain and managed to move, curling down against a barrel that was tied firmly in place.

I felt utterly broken and helpless.

"I would rather die," I thought despairingly. Then I immediately revolted against the idea. Why die? I might get well again. Perhaps I wasn't hurt very seriously and my wings were only tired and not broken. If I let them rest they might work again. If only I could escape those merciless scissors! Where was my cranny? What had become of my father and mother. My sister? Was the Trifler with her to the last?

And the terrible moment when I saw both of them plunge into the depths came back to my mind. It was shortly before my own fall. Where were they all now?

Then my thoughts grew confused; an irresistible drowsiness overcame me. I felt warm with the joy of being alive. Nothing ached now. But I could not move—I had no strength to raise my head, to stretch my legs.

"Scissors! . . . If only I could esc . . ."

I fell asleep and have no way of knowing how many hours I slept.

Imagine, then, my surprise and happiness when, waking up and feeling much stronger, I saw the Trifler a few steps away from me, peeping from behind another barrel! He was making signs to me the meaning of which I couldn't quite understand.

"My sister?" I couldn't help shrieking.

"Hush! Lie down quietly, rest, get your strength together, but pretend you are very ill—that is our only chance of being saved. Your sister is here and, thank goodness, she is unhurt. What a night we had! But cheer up, I have made some observations already and we seem to have had good luck," said the Trifler.

The sun was rising; the sea began to calm down. Only two men were now on deck; one was a tall old man, wearing a raincoat and a red fez, the other was half naked, barefooted, and his oily red fez had a long black tassel. The old man stood on a small high bridge and looked through the binoculars. The other sat on one of the rope piles and filled his pipe as he yawned and stretched himself lazily.

"All the others are asleep," the Trifler whispered. "If only we were strong enough to fly! But as it is, there is nothing to be done. Patience, my friend, patience."

"Where are we?"

"We are on a ship carrying pilgrims to the Holy Land, and that is very lucky. These people are very kind hearted and they are going almost in the same direction as we. The ship is bound for Jaffa. I found it out from the captain himself."

The Trifler probably had learned of the ship's destination, but the information certainly did not come from the captain himself. His natural bent for lying and boasting of his eminent connections never deserted him, even in the critical situation in which we found ourselves.

"I am terribly thirsty," I said.

"You can reach that wet rope over there; suck it. It is drenched by the rain so the water is fresh, though it may smell a bit of grease and tar. But it won't hurt."

I did as the Trifler suggested and moistened my feverish tongue and throat. Now I realized how hungry I was. If only I could have a small bit of some food! I felt I would have been content even with a dead fish! But there was nothing about that looked like food and I had to endure the ordeal patiently.

Meantime, with the sunrise, more people appeared

on deck, and among them were some women and children. They all made the sign of the cross and gazed wistfully eastward.

"Where are our crannies," said an old woman, looking around.

They all gathered about us. Now for the first time I saw my sister. An old man in long black garments had taken her into his arms and was stroking her lovingly. Every now and then my sister would attempt to pinch his hand, but he would draw it away.

"Don't do that," the Trifler told her. "It's a bad policy."

"Look at this one! He seems to be in worse shape than any of them," another man in black said of me. "Poor fellows, that terrible storm drove you away from shore!"

"It's a wonderful thing!" said the old man who still held my sister in his arms. "Verily it was the hand of Divine Providence! A shoreless sea and this small speck of a ship floating in the storm waters. Yet the Almighty has shown His boundless mercy to these creatures, driven by the stormy elements, tired, helpless, and doomed as they were, and has brought them right here to this ship as into a harbor of peace and salvation."

"The All Wise!" sighed another man in black.

"Crannies, our dear crannies," the children lisped.

A little tow-headed girl squatted down and stroked me tenderly.

The Trifler, who had apparently recovered more rapidly than we, rose to his feet and shook out his wings.

"Oh!" A little boy jumped away frightened.

"Don't be afraid of him. He's a nice birdy."

Our Trifler bowed gracefully to the right and left and performed, or rather tried to perform, the most elegant of his steps. But he couldn't and all but fell over on the deck. His fatigue was still great and his legs failed him.

The onlookers, however, seemed to appreciate his gallant efforts. They all laughed, including the black sailor who showed his dazzling white teeth as he chortled. And the old captain, who was watching the scene from his high bridge, shouted briskly: "Why don't you give the new passengers something to eat? Hey! Bring some cooked rice from the kitchen!"

How sensible that was! How clever! How timely!

"Let's feed the crannies, our new passengers. Ha, ha, ha!" one heard from every side.

We became the center of general attention. But there was nothing unfriendly in the demonstrations of this crowd. On the contrary, they all looked at us so lovingly and fondly!

"If they were roasted on a spit they'd make a fine meal—good soup, too." A thunderbolt had struck us and we turned cold with terror. And from a dark hatchway, as if from under the ground, appeared a brutish figure in a white cap and apron. Two frightful knives hung at his belt, and if it hadn't been for the cup of excellent rice that this individual held in his hands, his whole make-up would have personified mercilessness and death. But the rice—the rice softened that impression somewhat, and that wonderful rice was placed entirely at our disposal.

Frightened as we were, we were too hungry not to eat, and began at once, keeping an eye on the man with the knives. The latter lit his pipe and, standing with his legs wide apart, continued: "Yes, they'd make a fine roast."

"But does one eat them?" questioned a thin woman

with a baby in her arms. "Herons can't be eaten. They live on impure food."

"These are cranes, not herons. It's an altogether different breed," explained a rather decent-looking man with spectacles on his long nose.

That was better! The impudence of taking the noble cranes for nasty herons! It was more than we could stand, and if we didn't protest it was only because we were so completely taken with the rice.

The question as to whether our flesh was suitable or unsuitable for food affected us profoundly. We realized that it was of critical importance to us. Still our pride was stung when someone asserted confidently that our flesh, though eatable, was tough and tasted badly.

"It should be pickled first," slipped off my tongue.

"Teach them! You fool!" The Trifler nudged me in the side.

Fortunately my indiscretion bore no consequences. The suggestion that our flesh be tried was taken as a joke. Nobody ever thought of doing us any harm. We seemed to be entirely under the protection of the old man who had spoken about Divine Providence. And it was his intention to set us free as soon as he stepped on land.

"God himself has saved and maintained them. It is not for us to go against His holy will. Let His will be done," he said.

"Amen," came from his fellow pilgrims.

So our fate was settled.

As the ship moved we listened to the stories that the people told one another. We heard them say that it happens that whole flocks of different birds are driven to the ships during storms; that thousands of swallows were once driven to this same hospitable ship and safely taken ashore; that a ravaging vulture had also found refuge here once and would have been left in peace if he had not basely torn to pieces a tame pigeon, the captain's pet. The evildoer certainly well deserved capital punishment—he was shot!

And the time passed very pleasantly.

The only thing that worried and grieved us was that we were the only three who had been so happily saved. What had happened to the others? Where were they? Had they perished or had Divine Providence protected them as well? Maybe they were now on the deck of another ship or down on some island.

"The clouds were going from east to west," the Trifler reflected as he made some calculations. "We were caught by the storm halfway between Larnaka and Beirut. If the wind hadn't changed since, see what might have happened. In this direction lie endless waters. Our cranes might have passed the very mouth of the Nile and, unable to stop there, been carried farther by the wind. That certainly would have been terrible!"

"Yes, it would be terrible!" my sister squeaked.

But I never thought of these terrible things. The words about Divine Providence, spoken by the old man, took root in my heart. I became thoroughly convinced that our birds had been saved, and I closed my eyes, plunging into a dream. With great satisfaction I felt my strength returning to me after luncheon and a rest.

The ship rocked slightly and more sails were unfurled. A great cool shadow from the sails now covered the deck. The sounds of wonderful chords played on some strange divine instrument reached us from below. The people seemed so good and kind that they had made us forget those other wicked ones who had fired at us in the shallows of the Dnieper.

"Jaffa!" someone shouted from the fore part of the ship.

"Jaffa!" the Trifler interpreted to us.

Awakened by the sound of their cries, I saw the Trifler walking importantly up and down the captain's bridge, performing elaborate steps and generally behaving himself with the greatest familiarity.

The sailors, watching him, laughed amiably.

I felt that my strength was now completely restored. I woke my sister and we began pacing up and down the deck, stalking over the coiled rope piles and even over the extended legs of the passengers, who were sleeping on rugs strewn over the deck and enjoying the cool shadow made by the billowing sails.

When the Trifler caught sight of us he jumped down from the bridge and joined us.

"Now," he said, "don't dawdle. We have rested sufficiently. Fortune has smiled upon us. But one should abuse neither fortune nor Divine Providence. The people are kind to us. But their disposition may change at any time. The coast is near. See that white surf over there? Beyond it stretches a sandbank. There's a lighthouse on it. One, two, three! Follow me! God be with us!"

We never hesitated for a moment and, following the Trifler's example, skipped, flew through the widest space in the ship's rigging and rose into the air.

We heard someone on the ship shout: "Our crannies have flown away!" Then followed the sound of a child's cry. I turned my head and saw the pilgrims crowding to the edge, and high above their heads rose the thin hand of the old man sending us a benediction.

I swallowed my tears. How good people can be when they like! Why don't they want to be good all the time!

It's much safer to keep away from them!

CHAPTER XVI

OARING high in the air, we had instinctively turned away from Jaffa. We kept to the right and, crossing the surf, came down on the sands. A white marble foun-tain in a grove of skimpy palm trees was visible some distance away. A swarthy woman with a baby sat in the shadow and a tall earthen pitcher filled with water stood near by. Other women with exactly similar pitchers could be seen in the background. Farther off bells tinkled and clouds of reddish dust rose. This was a camel caravan with mounted guardsmen.

All this seemed to us unusual and interesting.

As soon as we landed, the rogue of a Trifler proposed that we elect a leader. He knew very well that it was his undeniable right to lead, but as our laws required the electoral procedure, he insisted upon it. Very plainly, he was eager to experience the thrill of being elected.

We voted and the Trifler was "unanimously" elected our leader. As to himself, he voted for me.

"Now, my friends, will you please pledge me absolute obedience?" our new leader said to us. "I have to demand it even from you, my queen," and he bowed playfully to my sister. "In the first place, my friends, note that we are three in number—that means that we can form a triangle. Whereas, if there were only two of us, it would have been impossible."

And the Trifler began to draw something on the sand to prove this incontestable point.

"You and I," he said to me, "will take turns at night watch and at the foreposts of the triangle. You, my lady, are free of these strenuous duties."

According to our laws, this was downright "arbitrary administration," but I found it better to say

168

nothing about it, and my sister was still less inclined to object.

The Trifler soon made himself familiar with the new locality and seemed to be on firm ground in planning our next stretch. He announced that our next flight would be made "along the seacoast direct to Port Said, Damietta, and the Nile." Then he proposed that we make a short trial flight. "In the first place, to get away from this fountain where the people keep coming, and in the second, to see if our wings have fully regained their strength."

We flew for about two hours and descended to a shallow near a dreary and desolate shore.

Towards evening we felt sufficiently rested. Our impatience to reach the Nile, where we hoped at least to learn something of the fate of our parents and friends, was so great that we decided to try to make this stretch during the night.

We formed into line, the Trifler leading, my sister and I following.

A wonderful, warm, starry night enveloped the sleepy earth. It was so splendid to feel this restored freedom! It was such incomparable happiness! Oh, if only our friends were safe!

169

The Trifler told us lies throughout the journey.

He told us that the captain had urged him to stay on board and accept a position as his assistant; but that he had refused it, referring to his high post as leader of a triangle; that the captain had shaken his claw, wishing him godspeed, and had finally kissed him, begging the Trifler not to forget him, and to call again if circumstances permitted.

" 'The entire ship and all the rice is at your disposal,' said the captain. 'As to the cook, don't mind him. Though he is a negro, he is thoroughly civilized and would certainly never dare to pickle the best friend of his captain.' "

We both laughed heartily and pretended to be-

lieve all his stories. The Trifler felt encouraged and went on. He declared that the captain had ordered a pair of genuine crane wings for himself somewhere in England, since he intended to join the cranes after his retirement and hoped that the Trifler would use his influence to help him make proper connections among us.

Toward dawn we noticed a glowing spark ahead of us, now visible, now disappearing. It was the lighthouse of Port Said, built far out into the sea.

We cranes can generally see the lighthouses from great distances, and at night the effect is most misleading. One sees the light and thinks it is quite near, but in reality one must fly and fly, apparently endlessly, before one reaches it. So it was this time; it was full daylight when the tower of a lighthouse emerged dimly visible in the distance. A great number of steamers and ships rocked on the waves, awaiting their turn to enter the harbor. Small, gayly whistling tugs and motorboats glided to and fro.

To the left was the arrow-straight line of a canal. A few, colossal vessels were moving slowly, leaving columns of black smoke behind.

Beyond Port Said stretched a lowland; it was partly grown with reeds, partly covered by yellow sands and a net of water streams. The air was peculiarly damp. A sandhill separated the lowland from Port Said.

"Delta! Delta of the Nile!" The Trifler pointed it out to us. "It begins here!"

Our hearts began to beat violently. Fear and hope alternately took possession of us. Now we pictured the joy of reunion. Then the sad prospect of orphanage and bitter memories.

We had taken a rest on the sandhill, and at noon started up the Delta, our eyes incessantly searching the spaces below and to the sides.

"Here!" the Trifler called joyfully.

We saw a small group of cranes resting on the shore of a lazy water stream.

We rushed toward them so hastily that we forgot all about discipline and broke the formation of our triangle. Those below answered our shouts with cheering trumpet calls.

These were some of our own—not from our former triangle, but from our caravan that had suffered the storm. Of the seventy cranes forming their triangle, only sixteen had survived. They had been miraculously saved, driven by the wind directly to these regions. What a stretch! The rest, they said, had been lost in the sea. There had been no news from them—most likely they had perished.

With sinking hearts we asked about Papa the Clarion. But the cranes knew nothing of him and his triangle, and they were still too weary from their forced flight to start on a search. They invited us to join them.

"Who is your leader?" the Trifler asked haughtily.

Then he stalked toward their leader and began talking to him in a low voice. He then persuaded us to move camp. For some reason he disliked the place and proposed another that in my opinion was exactly

173

identical. Then, at his suggestion, we selected from our midst a trustworthy reconnoitering detachment, which was to start its activities with the coming dawn.

Toward evening a few more cranes arrived. They too had survived by mere chance. One of them said he had seen Papa the Clarion still alive and struggling gallantly against the hurricane. This had been only a few moments before he himself was saved. Our hopes grew.

The day had just begun to glimmer when our scouts started. I had to take part in the search independently as a representative of our triangle, which had now grown considerably in size as the Trifler immediately incorporated every newcomer into it.

On the whole, I must say that our young leader was far more energetic and resourceful than the others, and some of the cranes gazed not without envy upon us.

I had taken a companion and we set off in quest of our dear ones. Hardly had we taken a few wing flaps when I noticed two large greenish-black objects lying on the sand under the blazing sun. I took them for two logs thrown on the shore by the waves, as their surface seemed to be somewhat moldy. But to my dismay these logs began to move, then crawled along, leaving deep furrows behind them in the sand. One of them yawned and showed terrible jaws with rows of sharp teeth. So huge were these jaws that they could have held not only a whole crane but a couple of pelicans. Neither my companion nor I knew what sort of monsters these were and there was no one to ask.

First, we circled around the immediate vicinity of our camp. Then we began to take in a wider range. Then, on a small densely grown islet we saw a group of cranes and among them was my dear, my precious papa, the Clarion, never more beloved than now.

I tumbled down, catching at something with my feet and sticking my beak into the ground. And, choking with happy tears, I was only able to say: "Papa, my papa!"

Papa trembled and stared at me without noticing my emotion.

"And your sister?" he asked me in a broken voice.

"She is with me and so is the Trifler. He has acted as our leader." I hurried to tell him all the news.

"As leader?" Papa pronounced, shaking his head

sorrowfully. "That is fine, very fine. And I can lead no longer. It must be my age. . . . I have ruined almost the whole triangle. I was over-confident. I never listened to wise counsels. . . . But I am glad, very glad, that you at least are alive!"

I gazed at Papa intently. Sorrow and exhaustion had changed him beyond recognition. Then I began looking around.

"Don't look for her—she has perished!" said Papa.

Only now did I fully grasp the whole meaning of his loss and ours!

And I began to weep bitterly.

"My poor sister! How shall I give her this unhappy news!"

Papa approved of our reconnoitering efforts. "That is the right thing to do," he said, and only deathly fatigue prevented him from making common cause with us. But he made a detailed inquiry as to the location of our camp and promised to come over to us with the faithful remnants of his triangle.

When I returned to camp at night I saw what had been accomplished during the day—about a hundred cranes had been assembled there, and this was without taking into account the parties that were too tired to move. Now our place looked something like a real crane camp.

We spent three days in flying about these regions, collecting the scattered parties.

On the second day Grandsire Longnose arrived with his unbroken triangle. With him it had been sheer luck. He had made the flight to Beirut on the day following our departure and it had gone off with complete success.

If only we had tarried another twelve hours! Oh, how wonderful it would have been! So many lives would have been saved! But who could know what was awaiting us? God alone—let His holy will be done!

They reckoned that about two hundred cranes from different triangles had been lost in the sea. It was fully a third of the whole army! The figure was shocking!

At the end of the third day the first columns of the Wise Wing Flap, who had continued to fly along the coast, arrived.

Now our elders began the reorganization of the army.

The Trifler had been legalized in his status as

leader. They were planning to form a triangle for him from the fragments of those who had lost their leaders. The Trifler certainly missed no chance to color his exploits brilliantly. But more weight was attached to my sister's testimony and to mine.

Now our brave leader suddenly found himself in a rather awkward position.

My sister and I, according to our family laws, had to remain in our papa's triangle. The Trifler was loath to part with us, or, to be exact, with my sister. Now he faced the dilemma—either to resign his leadership and stay with us, or to part from us. He didn't hesitate long and the languishing glances cast at him by my sister only hastened his decision.

"It is true," said our brave companion, "that leadership is a great honor and it is flattering to be a leader at my age, though there's no doubt that I fully deserve it. But it's not going to run away from me. My merits will always find their due. Meantime, I hope, our dear pap—I beg your pardon, sir; I meant to say, our honorable Mr. Clarion—I hope you will have no objection to my presence in your triangle, where under your benevolent patronage——"

Papa answered only with a rather dry, short "You

may stay," and the question was happily settled to our common satisfaction.

Old Longnose was greatly grieved over the loss of our dear, thoughtful, busy mamma and tried to comfort his bereaved friend as best he might.

"There is no sorrow in this life that time will not soften—that will fail to give way to new joy, as death itself gives way to new life," he said.

As for me, I became so attached to my dear Uralian cranny that the Trifler advised me to ask to be transferred to her triangle. But the Wise Wing Flap arranged the whole thing in the best possible way. One evening he came to us with Blackneck and, laughing outright, said to Papa the Clarion. "Hey, friend! Take this little fool into your triangle for a cure, will you? She's terribly sick, has no appetite, suffers from sleeplessness and so on, and I'm sure she'll recover in your triangle. I know this illness. It was long ago— very long ago—since I suffered from it. Still, I remember the symptoms and I wish you would take this child under your protection."

Papa assented, and since that evening my Uralian cranny, my beautiful Blackneck, and I have never been parted.

CHAPTER XVII

VEN on the lower Nile we were safe from the frosts and it seemed as if we might have stayed there till spring. But because there were too many people about, we continued our flight farther south. We moved in leisurely fashion, stopping now on the right, now on the left bank of the Nile, looking at and learning all about the marvels of this country of a glorious past.

The older cranes, who had been there many times, explained everything that we saw. They recounted to us historical events, whose stories had been handed down through many crane generations, and told us of their own recollections of this country.

Strange as it may seem, the Trifler lied much less. He became an attentive listener and a keen observer, and there seemed to be a perfect understanding between him and my sister. Blackneck and I were also very happy, and our trip might have been a blissful one had it not been for the many disturbing calamitous experiences we encountered. But I'd better follow the order of our travel.

The first wonder on our way was Cairo—a remarkable city with flat roofs, beautiful buildings, and a unique view of the Nile.

The Trifler showed me the gilded roof of a high minaret from which on a memorable occasion he had dispersed the swallows and the pigeons.

The streets were dark and narrow, but they were crowded and full of life. People in white and brightly colored garments thronged the roofed bazaars and the squares, and sat in picturesque groups in the shadows of trees, drinking something from tiny cups and smoking their long pipes.

Women with veiled faces strolled along the streets or drove by in their light carriages, chirping like the swallows that were seen flying by millions over the city.

Some birds, similar to us cranes, roamed the streets unafraid. These were ibises, still closer friends of man than our storks, who also were seen here in great numbers. But what beauties these ibises were! When we first saw them they were standing erect in a line along a shoal bank. Then, frightened, they rose and, stretching to their full length, looked in the sultry evening air like giant flame-red crosses. They are much larger birds than we, their necks are much longer, and their beaks are altogether different from ours, being rather short, solid, and curved in the form of a spoon.

We made a few trips to the sands on the left bank of the Nile and saw the majestic rows of pyramids. We saw a colossal stone head with human features, the nose broken and flattened; its strange headgear made it look as if huge ears were hanging on either side. The head was sticking out of the sands, giving the impression that the rest of the body must be buried underground. The whole thing was so enormous that, compared with it, not only the people but the camels too seemed like gnats. We saw the tall date trees and how cleverly the people climbed up to their thick crowns to get the clusters of ripe, savory fruits. The ground was strewn with dates, so that we couldn't help eating them, as well as some of those growing on the trees, since it was great fun to pluck them.

Desolate and dead, the sand deserts stretched beyond the pyramids. But no, there was life even there. Dark-skinned people in floating white cloaks sped on the backs of the light-footed camels; strings of caravans moved along and, soaring in the air, the great birds of prey of these lands—the buzzards—kept a vigilant eye on the level sands, seeking dead animals.

Once, at night, when a full moon poured its cool light over the silent desert, we noticed an animal with a beautiful, abundant mane; it moved with the light gait of a cat, casting a long shadow on the sands. Then came another shadow, and an animal almost exactly like the first, but without the mane, appeared. They met, snuffed at each other, and waved their tails.

"These are lions—the most ferocious of all the animals," the Trifler whispered to us. "Even the people fear them, and when they begin to roar it is like distant thunder! Most awe inspiring! We cranes have no need to fear them, but I would advise the people and the other animals to avoid them."

Later, we heard the roaring of the lions many times at night, and the howling of their servile attendants, the despised jackals, those vilest of all animals— cowardly thieves.

"That is nothing," Longnose said to us when, having returned from our excursions, we would describe to him what we had seen. "Wait till you get to the upper Nile and the Blue Mountains and the great lakes like seas."

We looked forward with impatient expectation to that moment.

And the dazzling natural beauties of the south, together with all the amazing sights of those regions, blotted from our memory the image of our homely native marshes. . . . Ingrates! We had forgotten our country!

When I say "we," I mean the young birds. As for our elders, they gathered together, counting the days until we should return; their conversation revolved constantly about our marshes. They tried to picture to themselves what was going on there, and when they spoke of it they said "at home," and they alluded to the lovely country in which we found ourselves as "here, on the Nile."

On our third stretch along the Nile we saw the ancient ruins and monumental statues of the Memnons. They were seated monsters, gaunt and devoid of all beauty, with only a distant likeness to men. Reflected in its shallows, they guard the Nile. Farther away were thick crowns of palms rising above the water in the form of bouquets. There we also saw a colonnade, the straight outlines of a half-ruined arch, and the needles of the obelisks. All these were traced with a fanciful pattern of mysterious age-old inscriptions.

I was particularly fascinated by these inscriptions. Without actually knowing it, I felt that these were more than mere ornaments. On one occasion I was leaning and musing over a fallen fragment of a cornice. I was all alone, everything around was quiet, and I was lost in meditation. I contemplated the mysterious signs on the cornice and tried to penetrate their meaning.

"Hey, you, young philosopher!" a voice sounded near me.

I started.

"Don't you forget, my dear, that these are not the Ostashkovo Marshes," said Longnose, tapping me on the back. "Look out there. See that crocodile and how covetously he's eying you? Why are you dreaming over this stone? Did you find something that interests you?"

I told him what occupied my thoughts.

Longnose looked at the inscription, then, as if recalling something, said to my keen satisfaction: "Yes, of course, that's very simple."

"Dear Grandfather, please explain!"

"Well, you see that first sign? What does it look like?"

Now I saw very plainly that the first sign was an attempt on the part of an unknown ancient artist to draw a lion. Though the drawing was faulty and childish, the lion was unmistakably recognizable.

The Trifler and my sister joined us. Then more wings flapped near by—it was Papa, and with him were five more cranes. My Blackneck also arrived— she loved to hear Longnose. In a word, our eminent professor had quite an audience assembled before him. And it seemed to please him.

REFLECTED IN ITS SHALLOWS, THEY GUARD THE
NILE

"Well," he continued, "lion. Remember its first letter?"

"*L*," said Blackneck, and grew confused.

"Why not Z, Blackneck?" teased one of our cranes.

"No fooling!" Papa stopped him. "Go ahead, friend; this is most interesting. Let us go on. Lion. We have it. A lion it is!"

"The second sign is a peculiar-looking shaft with a pyramidal top, such as we have seen in this country."

"Obelisk," I guessed.

"Let us remember O."

"Third?"

Here several cranes, scanning the drawing, exclaimed, "Nail!"

"Right! The fourth sign is again an animal. I believe you all know him by his horns—it's a goat; so the fourth letter is *G*; then——"

But here we all shouted in chorus, "Nose," and began looking at one another in stupefaction.

What was it? A coincidence, or——

Our venerable grandsire stood with bowed head as if in mute respect before a passing sacred memory.

"Grandfather, it is you. It is your name. How is that?" My sister asked timidly.

"No, it is not mine. It must be that of one of my forbears—our Longnose family is one of the most ancient among the cranes. But it is strange, very strange, and I certainly never expected it!"

Our wise but modest old gentleman was positively embarrassed by his discovery. It certainly did seem extraordinary that I should have stopped precisely before this piece of stone, that Longnose should have found me, and that the audience should have assembled to hear the marvelous interpretation!

We were all elated over our discovery and prouder than ever of our leader.

"Here! Here!" We heard the voice of the Trifler who had disappeared during the first moments of our bewilderment.

We thought he had found something interesting and we all rushed to him. We found him standing with his beak touching the sand, as if he were examining something attentively.

On the smooth surface of the sand we saw some signs which were the object of the Trifler's scrutiny.

"What do you think, gentlemen? Could this figure be taken for a tree?" he asked.

"Why," I said, "all right. Let us suppose it is a tree."

"The next sign is an animal—see its upper lip?—it's a rhinoceros; the next is——"

"Ivy!" Somebody screamed.

Here we all burst into such merry laughter that even our old Longnose couldn't help joining us.

"Isn't he the limit! Ha, ha, ha!" My papa's roaring laughter dominated everything.

"I was so afraid," my sister said in a low voice, "that you were in earnest and wanted to fool us all, because you were jealous of our grandfather's well-deserved glory!"

"How could you think so! As if you didn't know me!" the Trifler remonstrated.

"Yes, sir!" Papa was still shaking with laughter. "If you want your name to be remembered, you'd better pick some solid material!"

"Nothing enduring is ever built on sand," the other cranes joked.

"You'd better get a nice hard stone and try to cut it deep. The sand will hold only till the first wind rises, or rather till the coming of the first sparrow who takes it into his head to walk here!"

"Or better yet, since it will endure longer than all the stones taken together," interjected the Wise Wing Flap, who came on the scene attracted by our merry voices, "the best material of all is a crane's heart or anyone's heart. Let your good and glorious deeds be so deeply engraved in the hearts of your contemporaries that their ineradicable impression may be handed down without monuments that are perishable, however imposing they may be—handed down through generations to posterity so that they may glory in their kind, wise ancestors. Friend Longnose, accept my heartfelt congratulations!"

After some games and dances in honor of our esteemed old leader, we started to the other side of the river, for a bath, but on our way we came upon such a distressing scene as changed our plans.

In the high reeds along the river we noticed a group of horsemen; they did not inspire any alarm in us. They had no rifles and carried some bird prisoners on their hands; what sort of birds these were we couldn't make out, as their heads were covered with red hoods. Judging by their feathers, they were birds of prey and we didn't feel a bit sorry for them. These birds proved to be traitors and accomplices of man in his evil designs.

The tops of the reeds swayed and rustled, and a snow-white swan appeared, flapping his magnificent wings. He was rising in the air when the horsemen shouted and released their trained ruffians. Two hawks flashed through the air. One of them soared above the frightened swan, the other flew under him, cutting him off from the reeds and the water. The swan began to develop great speed, trying to get away from his pursuers. They raced after him and gained upon him. We saw it all and started to help the swan, but it was too late.

The hawk that was flying higher than the swan swooped down and struck him from above; we could hardly distinguish him, so closely did he cling to the beautiful white plumage. Another hawk attacked from below and we heard the swan's wailing cry in his death agony. Beating his bloodstained wings desperately, the swan plunged heavily to the ground, his enemies clinging to him.

The horsemen, shouting wildly, galloped toward him.

"Too late!" Papa said to us, for we were loath to give the swan up. "Turn back! We couldn't reach him in time to help him—we can do nothing now. Hey, young fellow, don't take any chances!"

The warning came just in time. The horsemen had caught sight of us and were pointing their hands in our direction. One of them jumped down and removed the hawks from their prey, then put the red hoods on their heads.

We flew away from the bank and over the river.

A tug crawled below, pulling two large boats full of armed soldiers in white helmets with light green veils. In the distance more such transports were seen and the whole flotilla of light, short-masted boats, with their unusually long, thin, flexible yards and sails, resembled enormous swallow wings.

CHAPTER XVIII

HE farther we flew up the Nile, the fewer people we saw. The character of the scenery was also changing. It was the time of year when the tropical heat reaches its peak of intensity. The nearness of the desert's burning sands increased the interminable heat of the torrid zone and scorched the sparse rich plantations.

"Only to think that they're having real winter back home now," Papa said. "There must have been some good frosts and everything is lying under deep snow. Only the sparrows and crows can stand it. If we stayed we should freeze to death!"

He explained to us the reason for our yearly migrations south and we thanked God who had given us powerful wings that we might enjoy everlasting summer.

But it was growing simply unendurable here. All extremities are equally bad; great frost and excessive heat are just as hard to bear. Farther south, they told us, it would be better. We would enter the region of thick forests and high mountains with snow peaks and glaciers and great lakes moderating the heat.

For a whole week we flew over the foaming, turbulent waters of the Nile, and occasionally saw unskillful navigators perish as their boats crashed against the rocks. Then we reached the point where the Nile divides into two—the wide stream of Atbara turns to the left, while Bahr-el-Abiad flows straight onward. The boggy mist-veiled shallows surrounded a city. It was Khartoum. We preferred to pass over it as quickly as we could for we heard sounds of shooting coming from that direction. Three races, we had been told, were fighting there: the black, the brown, and the white. What the fight was about we didn't know. The Trifler offered us his own explanation, but somehow it didn't sound altogether convincing.

He told us that the brown people, or Egyptians, objected to their neighbors being black but that there was no way of washing off their blackness. However, they would not leave it at that; they still were trying to find a way to bleach them. The white people from the north came here to help the Egyptians. They wanted pay for their services, but as the blacks remained black, the Egyptians refused. Then the whites decided to collect for themselves and all began to fight among themselves.

This was the version the Trifler gave us, but one cannot take it seriously.

Our own observations, however, confirmed one thing, that is, that the three races were continuously fighting.

Once when we flew over a great dark forest we heard voices below and saw human beings trailing through the jungle. Most of them were black, naked and half-naked people who were carrying on their heads and backs white tusks, pitchers of water, and bags of rice. Some of them were in chains. Brown people with whips goaded them along.

These strange travelers evidently knew nothing of the whites who were waiting for them on the outskirts of the jungle. But we saw it all and could not help feeling some gratification. "Wait," we thought, "until the whites meet you. They certainly will free the blacks and punish the browns for their cruelty."

We were right only in one point: as soon as the two parties saw each other they began to fight. Many were killed on both sides, but the whites won. Next morning we saw that some of the browns were hanged on trees. The rest, blacks and browns alike, carried the loads and the whites goaded them with whips. And everywhere in this country there were whole camps of the blacks burned by the whites and whole piles of white corpses.

To avoid such distressing sights, we veered off our route and at last, thank goodness, got away from all the people and reached a wilderness never trodden by white feet or brown.

What wonderful forests grew here! What giants of the tree kingdom lifted their crowns, casting enormous shadows over the great spaces!

What marvelous meadows we saw in the jungle, where quiet streams moved slowly toward Bahr-el-Abiad that flowed through the wilderness, cutting it in two!

Few were the huts of the blacks on their fields of wheat or rice, and few the boats on the river. The fewer, the better!

We had caught sight of a meadow suitable for our halt, but before gliding down we circled it many times as a measure of precaution. The meadow was near a palm forest that swarmed with monkeys and parrots. The hour was just before sunset. Since, in these parts, thick darkness follows immediately upon brilliant sunlight, flocks of parrots were already settling down for their night's rest. Beyond the forest was a great lake, its shores covered by a dense growth. Several streams linked the lake to the river. From one side of the lake dull splashes were audible and the heavy sniffing of massive black bodies—these were hippopotamuses—ungainly monsters, clumsy on the ground but nimble swimmers and divers.

On the outskirts of the forest grew a lonely tree with a mass of light roots growing from its branches above ground. A strange animal once approached this tree; its body was rather small, its legs were as long as those of a camel, it had an unusually long neck, a small head with short horns, and lovely black eyes.

"That's a giraffe," Longnose said to us, "a peaceful and lovable animal that harms no one. I can see the danger threatening her right now and I shall warn her. . . ."

Longnose invited Papa to go with him and they both rose suddenly and flew to the giraffe, touching her with their wings as they passed by.

They were just in time. The frightened giraffe leaped aside and ran away. Crawling along the trunk of the lonely tree appeared a huge snake; it wriggled loose for a moment, then coiled itself about the tree and disappeared under the thick growth of the roots.

Night in these regions was full of lurking perils. The terrible darkness hindered the sentinels' task, for the moon was on the wane and appeared only after midnight.

With nightfall myriads of glowworms appeared everywhere—now motionless in the grass, now flying. A pair of round, greenish dots flashed from time to time in the jungle. An uneasy commotion was heard among the monkeys, frightened by a panther. On the shoals crocodiles stirred. The surface of the lake was bright with the reflection of the starry sky. Heavy figures appeared against this bright background— these were the elephants who had come to water. We had first seen them while it was still daylight; they were running through the jungle, apparently in great irritation, for they drew in the air through their trunks and then blew it out with a sharp sound like a steamer whistle.

We soon realized by the splashing of the water and the rustling of the reeds that the elephants had decided to have a swim. The dark orange disc of the rising moon appeared above the horizon, and presently its radiant light illumined the crest of the jungle trees.

What a lovely scene! What immeasurable, unending grandeur in creation!

But a fearful tumult, breaking out in the forest, made us rise instantly and dash away.

The clamorous yell of a panther sounded and the uneasy shrieks of the monkeys. A general agitation and commotion followed! Wails and moans could be heard as if someone were calling for help. The elephants rushed through like hurricanes, smashing everything in their way. Farther and farther we flew and only with the dawn did we descend to rest.

No, you cannot sleep here as quietly as in our peaceful northern marshes. You feel drowsy and tired.

Constant perils day and night wear you out. You would like to fall asleep instantly, but look out! The crocodiles are stealing in near us. And our only trust is in the vigilance of our wary watchmen!

Here it is day rather than night that brings rest and relaxation. And we had to change our northern habits in order to adapt ourselves to the new environment.

And I began to understand now why we hatch our children in the north. Here one can think of nothing but one's own safety, let alone the strenuous duties of hatching and rearing. I wondered how the native species managed it, but then, since they were native they probably know better than we—passing travelers.

And our elders were right when they said, "back home," in speaking of the north. Now even we young birds began to realize the meaning of those words, and the bewitching beauties of southern climes began to lose their fascination for us.

CHAPTER XIX

HERE was no question of food along the Nile. We found it in abundance everywhere, but there were very few places where we could rest undisturbed. Proceeding by easy stages and discovering a safe retreat, we would sometimes stop there for whole weeks.

At last the faint, soft contours of the mountains appeared before us. First we took them for clouds. Think how high these mountains must have been, since we caught our first glimpse of them a week before we reached them!

203

The glaciers covering their summits were to us unattainable. Even the eagles and the buzzards could barely reach them. Great was our astonishment, therefore, to see an object of peculiar form flying beyond the clouds on a level with the glaciers.

It was a sort of bladder and it must have been very large, though to us it looked no bigger than a radish. Below a basket was tied.

We were quick to realize that only human genius could construct a thing like that. Yes, it was the people to whom God, for the sake of our peace and safety, gave no wings! The people, destined to creep over the earth, were invading the regions belonging to us. Poor birds!

Flying for five days through the mountain passes, we managed to cross several ridges and reached the farther side of the range. There lay the boundless watery plains of an inland lake on whose shores we were to stay till it was time for us to return home.

Home! What a wonderful word!

"Isn't it strange, dear, that they don't have cranberries here?" Blackneck said to me. "I was looking for them all over but couldn't find a single berry! Here, with all the abundance and variety of vegetation! And they say that you can get anything here!"

"No, madam," the Trifler laughed, "you will find no cranberries here. The natives have not yet attained that stage of perfection. Cranberries have far too delicate a taste to be appreciated by savages!"

"That's too bad," and Blackneck shook her wings. "It seems as if I'd gladly give up all the dates, bananas, and nuts for a cranberry!"

"Why on earth do women always want something that you can't get them!" I thought. "I must try to distract her in some way."

But Blackneck was already consoled. She had found a ripe cocoanut that had fallen down, splitting in two as it struck against a stone, and thrusting her beak in, she drank its milk with visible relish.

Not far from our camp there was a settlement of blacks. A high picket fence surrounded a group of huts. These were round as barrels, coated with clay, and had high cone-shaped roofs. Their maize fields lay all about, also guarded by fences. Cattle pens occupied the spaces between the fields and the huts, and the fences surrounding these were higher still, while prickly plants, with thorns much longer than our beaks, were stuck on the picket points. This was a measure of precaution against panthers and lions.

The people living in this village went about naked; they carried no rifles and were therefore not so dangerous. I say "not so dangerous," because danger still existed. They were archers so dextrous and skillful in aiming their short javelins that we couldn't feel quite safe in their vicinity.

Two of our cranes had already paid the death penalty for their over-confidence. We were mourning their loss. But what was more surprising than the death of the two young birds—Uncle Kloo-Kloo, old as he was and a crane of the world, poor fellow, he too fell a victim to his carelessness. A sharp arrow pierced him under my very eyes, and a black man carried him triumphantly into his hut.

When the men would go away for a while and only women and children were left in the village it was quite safe to explore their cornfields and we certainly didn't wait for an invitation to do so.

Even here the storks made their nests on the roofs. But there weren't so many of them and we lived in friendship together. From them we learned many things about the blacks.

These storks are somewhat different from ours.

They are smaller in size and they live in these regions all year round keeping close to the human habitations, which is a matter of necessity in winter time.

"The winter here is merely rain, rain and rain, which is interrupted only by violent storms. And if it weren't for the people, we should sometimes feel lost," they said.

We also made the acquaintance of the giant marabous. What lovely birds they are! They have such magnificent feathers that the people are constantly robbing them. What's the use, after all, of wearing beautiful plumage?

The men usually came back heavily laden with booty, consisting mostly of elephants' tusks which they piled near their cabins. Sometimes they would fill their heavy, clumsy boats with the tusks and row far out over the lake. The storks told us that on the opposite side lived people who took the tusks for other goods. When the blacks returned without the tusks they were generally in high spirits; they sang and danced and drank something from kegs. The women and children seemed to love such homecomings and they joined in the jubilation. They would dance and drink too, and bright kerchiefs would appear on their kinky heads, and all sorts of trinkets.

Once a small party of black men, returning from their hunting expedition, brought a prisoner along—a white man with his arms twisted behind his back. He looked very tired and could hardly stand on his feet.

The blacks gave him food and drink, untied his arms, and, leaving two sentinels at the entrance, locked him in one of the cow pens.

"Why did they ever bring him?" said an old marabou. "They ought to know that they can never hope to get away with it!"

At that time we didn't pay much attention to his words. But a few days later we were awakened at midnight by the crackling of flames, and saw fire devouring the huts, and heard shooting and shrieks of despair.

It was a party of whites who had surrounded the village and attacked its inhabitants. We never learned the fate of the white prisoner, but when the sun rose there was no trace of what had formerly been a village—only heaps of ashes remained.

The whites had taken with them as they departed all the tusks and the surviving cattle. We were now left as sole owners of the fields of ripe corn.

At first we found the new state of affairs very pleasant. It was like a continuous holiday and we enjoyed the quiet and the rich heritage that we shared only with the storks, who had lost their nests in the fire. But soon the unburied human corpses attracted such a number of all sorts of flesh eaters, four footed and winged, that their endless fighting and uproar made our stay intolerable.

Only after a few blacks, somehow spared by the raiders and the flames, had returned to the charred site to rebuild their huts, was quiet restored.

We felt sorry now that, believing them all to be dead, we had so recklessly devastated their fields!

We even forgave them the murder of Uncle Kloo-Kloo and our other friends, though somewhere at the bottom of our hearts we had a vague notion that it was precisely for that crime that God had punished them.

And once they were punished, it behooved us to receive them without rancor or resentment.

But this is just preaching. Try to receive them in

any spirit! The people were back, and back with them were their ill feelings.

With an angry hiss, an arrow flashed and pierced the earth a few steps from my Blackneck!

No! Decidedly, all the people—including the blacks—are equally hopeless.

 NCLE KLOO-KLOO had left a widow. She was a nice, spruce, middle-aged cranny and our papa had taken her under his protection. He became so absorbed in his new responsibilities that he could now spare far less time for us, saying that my sister and I were at an age where we no longer needed his guidance.

But Grandfather Longnose continued to devote most of his leisure to us. The dear gentleman had grown very old of late; he no longer went with us on our excursions. and often said that his only prayer to the merciful God was to grant him the happiness of seeing our dear Ostashkovo Marshes once more.

It was the end of February and, from the conversations of our elders, we gathered that the time of our return flight was near. And strange to say, the last days seemed endless; never yet had time dragged so slowly!

We began our first short stretches northward in the direction of Khartoum.

Toward the end of February we were all assembled in the vast marshes near the estuary of the Blue Nile.

Here we had to await the arrival of our parties that had been wintering along the upper Blue Nile in Abyssinia, and then we would start our homeward trip together.

"We shall rest here about a week and then God be with us," said Grandfather Longnose, and he sighed.

He had taken to sighing often of late, especially toward nightfall. It was with difficulty that he had made the stretches from the great lakes, and had often stayed behind, joining us again at the halts.

"Courage, old man," Papa said to him. "All you

need is a good rest, so let us stay here longer. I shall see to it that you have good nourishment and don't waste your strength in useless exertions. I am sure God will grant you strength to reach home!"

"I rather doubt it," Longnose sighed. "If only I could get up to Philae! If I cannot get home, I'd rather die there than any place else."

Needless to say, we all knew the reason why. It was in Philae that we had discovered the name of his ancestor written in hieroglyphics.

"It's a good thing we've left the great lakes—the rainy season has begun there already," the Wise Wing Flap said. "Only once in my life was I caught in them. There was an epidemic among our cranes and I stayed with the others to nurse our sick. It certainly was terrible! God save us from another such experience!"

But we were destined to suffer that ordeal.

Toward evening, on the fourth day after our arrival in the marshes of the Blue Nile, such a dense fog arose that we could see nothing a beak's length ahead of us.

Blackneck and I hid under a palm tree and decided to stay there till it cleared. We seemed to be all alone in the world. Then we heard the voice of the Trifler a short distance away.

"Hey!" he shouted. "Look out! Something evil is coming!"

"Stop your soothsaying! You frighten me!" Black-neck protested.

Indeed, there was reason to feel frightened. More oppressive than the fog were the brooding silence and the suffocating air charged with electricity.

We saw the sunset's red glow sink into black darkness. The first distant rumble of thunder sounded, and its dull peals were long in dying away.

A light wind fluttered over our heads. Then it thundered again; this time much nearer. The fog grew so dense that we no longer seemed to be surrounded by air but by water; and following upon the fresh thunderclap, torrents of rain came pouring over us.

"Help! I'm drowning!" we heard a moan.

But a great wave, coming from goodness knows where, overtook us. We made an effort to rise, but the force of the falling water paralyzed our wings and, after flying a few yards, we tumbled down—happily not to the ground, but to some thin, swaying intertwined branches. Struggling desperately with our wings and feet, we managed to preserve our balance on this rocking foothold. Below foamed cascades of water. The moment was critical.

But before we could draw a breath we were blinded by such a glare of lightning that what we had seen during the storm at sea was a mere flash by comparison. Then came such a crash of thunder that we lost both our senses and our wits.

When I recovered I was, alas, alone, being carried along by a stream. I struck against something, then was once more borne away, and finally I stuck in the reeds. Presently I gathered my strength together. The pouring torrents continued unabated. There was no wind and the cold waters fell vertically. It seemed a veritable deluge; it looked as if we should never see the sky again. The noise was such that when I tried to shout I could hardly hear my own voice.

It thundered continuously. The greenish glare of the lightning never died out. I was so exhausted that I had lost my powers of resistance; all my limbs were cold and rigid, and again I was carried away by a stream.

"This is the end!" flashed through my mind.

At last I touched firm ground and almost at the same time the torrents ceased abruptly. A strong gust of wind bore the darkness asunder; soon it was scattered and above my head I saw the constellation of the Southern Cross.

The wind gained in strength, and drove away the black clouds with their thunder, lightning, and torrential rain. The dying rumble of the tropical storm was still audible now and then.

"Thank goodness, I am alive! But my dear ones?" The beloved image of Blackneck rose before me. "Where is she?"

But a search before daylight was not to be thought of.

The rising sun warmed me and I began to stretch my limbs and move about. I was on a barren island without the least sign of vegetation. The first thing I saw were the open jaws of a crocodile slowly approaching me. I was on the verge of fainting, but I started and leaped aside. The hideous beast rose to its feet, champing its jaws angrily.

Happily the corpse of an antelope now attracted the monster's attention and I was saved.

In about two hours I felt rested, and vigorous enough to start in search of the others.

Soon I came upon a group of cranes who told me of their narrow escape from death. Several of them, who were less exhausted, joined in my quest. We rose in the air and began circling slowly about, gradually widening the range of our observations.

First of all I saw Papa the Clarion and the Widow Kloo-Kloo. I rushed to greet them. They were unharmed and, receiving some instructions from Papa, I lost no time in proceeding farther.

"Find our veteran first," Papa shouted as I was leaving; "that's the most important thing."

As to what was "the most important thing" in my search, I held a somewhat different view from that of my papa. The one most important to me I found only about noon. My Blackneck, thank goodness, was safe, but she was imprisoned by the bowlders near the river, and couldn't get free without help from outside.

"How hungry I am!" was the first thing she said to me.

Though I was unpleasantly struck by this childish egotism, the joy of seeing her was so great that I didn't even reproach her but led her to the bushes where we both had luncheon. Then we continued our search with redoubled zeal.

We saw a cranny who was flying rather low and looking anxiously from side to side. It was my sister.

"And the Trifler?" I shouted to her.

"I don't know," she replied, and began to cry.

We comforted her as best we could, and asked her to come along with us.

As we flew about we saw dead animals scattered here and there who had perished during the storm. There were also a few dead cranes and we went down to see if we could recognize them. Longnose and the Trifler were not among them.

"They must be safe somewhere," we decided. I felt little doubt that the Trifler—that brave, energetic, and quick-witted fellow—had found some way out of all the difficulties. But our aged, beloved grandsire Longnose caused us the gravest anxiety. And for greater efficiency in conducting the search we broke up into several parties.

As had been agreed, we all gathered at noon in a place indicated by Papa. About a dozen cranes were assembled there. But Papa was absent.

218

"He went to look for the old gentleman," Widow Kloo-Kloo told me. "He will not even eat before he finds him!"

Why, that was only natural!

"Here they come!" called several excited voices.

And really, by the characteristic wing flapping of the approaching cranes, we knew them to be Papa and Longnose. They flew close together and Papa supported the old gentleman as they came down.

Papa told us he had seen the Trifler who, upon learning that my sister was safe, had flown farther to assist the others.

"Isn't he horrid!" my sister said.

"No, he acted as a gentleman should," Longnose said to her reproachfully.

"I fully approve of the Trifler," agreed Papa.

And my sister seemed contented.

Toward evening we were all together again. Our loss this time was inconsiderable.

The Trifler came in last. He brought with him the fragment of a rug trimmed with gold braid, which, he asserted, proved conclusively that he had spent the night on the back of an elephant, from whose saddle he had torn the fragment as a souvenir. Our hero told us that, during the storm the night before, he had been carried away by the torrents but had never lost his presence of mind. He had dashed up at an opportune moment, and gropingly reached the top of a date-palm tree. First of all he had eaten a few dates; then he had plucked a whole cluster of them, intending to present them to my sister, but the palm struck by lightning had fallen with a loud crash. The Trifler had narrowly escaped the jaws of a crocodile; as a matter of fact his left leg had struck the crocodile's teeth. It was a terrible moment that he will never forget! Then, together with the palm, he had been borne along by a current and flung against a ship. He had heard the voices of people and smelled the smoke and soot. He had gone to the deck and moved close to the captain's cabin to hear what they were saying. But he realized the danger of his situation and stayed only a few moments to catch his breath. Then he had started to fly but was too worn out to withstand the torrents. He had fallen and struck the back of some powerful beast. Guessing at once by the tail that it was an elephant, he had climbed up. The Trifler had little doubt that the elephant belonged to some important official—in all

THERE WAS AN UNUSUALLY ELEGANT HOWDAH
ON THE ELEPHANT'S BACK

likelihood to the Governor of Khartoum himself, as there was an unusually elegant howdah on its back. The Trifler pulled down the curtains and settled himself comfortably for the rest of that terrible night. Only when the rain had ceased in the morning did he leave his retreat.

"I am infinitely sorry, my friend," he said to my sister, "that I did not bring you the date cluster as I intended, but if you knew the use I put it to, I'm sure you would approve."

"It was to me that the kind fellow gave his dates," Grandfather Longnose said. "I was totally exhausted, helpless, and hungry when he found me."

We were all deeply moved by the Trifler's generosity and kindness; his story was given full credence and the last doubts as to its truthfulness dissipated. We knew that a few things had been added to the tale, but we wanted to believe it and we did believe it.

One should be able to recognize the difference between a lie and a poetic inspiration. Anyone can lie who can quiet his conscience. But only a few chosen mortals can create stories and in such cases the truthfulness of the story is of no importance. The story should entertain you, it should amuse you and exalt your ideas, and that's all that's necessary.

There are unimaginative persons unable to rise above the commonplace, who are generally very fond of "investigating" things.

I am quite certain that several such persons, on reading of my travels will say: "How could he write it when cranes have no ink and no paper?"

Such a remark would show, to say the least, a total lack of humor. Take, for example, the Widow Kloo-Kloo who had now become my stepmother. Listening to the Trifler, she said: "Nothing but a pack of lies!"

But in her this is pardonable. She is known to be a person of more than limited intelligence and little education, and it was not for those qualities that my papa honored her with his attention. She is a good woman and has an excellent disposition. As to her critical remarks, why, I think even the most simple minded of the teals would attach no importance to them.

That evening, however, when the Trifler was talking to my sister, he frankly admitted that he didn't remember exactly what had happened to him during the night, but he believed that it was all about as he had told it to us and that there had been even more.

"But the dates?" my sister asked.

"The dates? In all honesty, the dates were there!"

That evening the day for our departure was definitely fixed.

CHAPTER XXI

HE next day we spent in preparations for the journey. These consisted of the organization of the separate units of our army and the election of leaders.

Grandsire Longnose resigned from his post as Supreme Guide, pleading great age and fatigue. And neither our vigorous protests nor supplications could make him change his decision. Papa the Clarion was unanimously elected his successor.

The Trifler was elected leader of a triangle. He received the news with the greatest composure and pretended that it was not only a natural but the only sensible thing that could have been done, and that he had expected it. And in a businesslike way he immediately counted those entrusted to him, thirty-two pairs of cranes.

Then he stated in brief the guiding principles of his future policy: "In my social and military duties during our homeward march I shall be fair but very strict. Apart from this, I want you all to regard me as your good old friend."

The most unexpected and exciting of all the election results was my own appointment as leader. The new office put me on a footing with the Trifler! At first I couldn't believe it, but the number of votes I had received was so overwhelming that there could be no doubt about it.

At that time I thought I owed the honor of my election to Papa's popularity. Later, I learned that the list of candidates was drawn up by Grandfather Longnose and his prestige was so great that his recommendations were regarded as sacred orders.

I made no speech. I only said I should try to emulate my papa's example in everything.

"With the exception of that one sea flight, I hope,"

Papa remarked. "I wish you would adopt as your motto, 'Better slow—but sure.'"

With the next dawn we started on our great journey northward. Soon we perceived the rolling plains of the sand deserts lying near the lower Nile. Our first night halt was near Wady-Halfa and it passed quietly and uneventfully.

My Blackneck showed me such careful consideration and kindness that I wondered whether it would have been the same if I had remained one of the rank and file among our cranes, without the halo of social distinction.

Two more stretches and we reached Philae with its time-honored ruins.

Grandfather Longnose's strength was ebbing. From the first stretch he was several hours behind us, and we had to make one halt more than was scheduled to give him a chance to catch up with us and to rest. As soon as he had reached Philae our old gentleman dropped to the ground and refused to continue the trip.

Gathered around our dying guide and leader, we spent a melancholy evening. Longnose lay beside the fragment of cornice bearing his name. The night was still and moonlit. The jackals howled on the other bank of the river and the red lights of the fishermen's boats twinkled in the darkness.

Our leader spoke to us.

"Live in peace. Live without wishing evil to any-one, and when treated evilly, do not seek revenge. Remember that all vengeance is futile, since it brings no consolation. Blame no one, since none of you is without blame. Always cling together. Your power is in unity. Remember that your duty to society, to the common cause, comes before your private affairs. Love—because love is everything—it is the mother of all earthly joys and delights. Love is stronger than death. And if I now die peacefully and well content, it is because I know that until my last breath I will follow you lovingly in my thoughts and will picture to myself your joy in seeing again our dear and wonderful country."

"I feel very sleepy," he added, hardly audible.

At dawn, when we were ready to depart, we saw our Longnose lying with his long legs outstretched and his tufted head under his wing.

We rose silently, and the silence remained unbroken during the whole stretch.

But here is Cairo. Here are the green plains of the Delta of the Nile, and here is the lovely blue streak of the Mediterranean!

All the sights seemed familiar. The plan of our journey was now etched quite clearly and distinctly in our minds. Our impatience carried us on, and, casting indifferent glances over all the beauties of the east, we dreamed of our home, of our marshy plains and hummocks dotted with bright flowers.

Reaching the mouth of the Danube, we parted with the legions of the Wise Wing Flap.

Moving it was to see the old leader bid good-bye to my papa. He said he knew it was his last journey.

"But, my friend, when one sees a death as beautiful and serene as that of our Longnose, one can only yearn to follow him."

"Come! Come!" said Papa. "You'll see. We shall fly together yet."

But the Wise Wing Flap was right. We never saw him again.

CHAPTER XXII

ITH breathless speed we flew cheerfully and boldly over the dark northern woods, blowing our trumpets joyfully. It was the end of March.

Snow was still visible here and there, but the weather was already warm and only the nights and the mornings were chilly. With every day it grew sunnier and warmer.

Then came April with its turbulent springtime streams, the first tinge in the grass, the first snowdrops. . . . We were near our goal.

A joyful experience was in store for us here. A new member joined our army. It was the captive crane who had heroically saved our Trifler.

He said he had grown quite tame and had won the confidence of the people so that they had ceased to clip his wings. He had spent the whole winter in a warm shed together with chickens and other domestic fowl. Toward spring he had once heard the people utter again the hateful word "scissors," and had decided to run away. His wings were now sufficiently grown so that he could make short flights, rising quite high over the fences and the roofs of the houses.

He waited for a favorable occasion and flew away.

First he lived for a while in a fir wood where he ran constant risks of freezing to death or of starving. His only food was last year's bilberries, frozen and blackened, that he had to dig out of the snow and the fir cones. Gradually, with the warm weather, more food appeared. Meantime his wings had grown longer and he kept on exercising them. That morning, when he heard the sound of our trumpets and saw us in the air, his strength had increased tenfold and he had rushed to us, catching up with the first triangle.

"You will not drive me away, will you, my friends? I would like to join your army for good."

Needless to say, he was most enthusiastically received and heartwarming cheers were given in his honor.

The meeting between the former prisoner and the Trifler was most moving.

Two or three more stretches of forced flying and we would be home at last!

That day we passed over Moscow. It was about midnight. The whole city, especially the churches, was brightly illuminated. Thousands of people crowded the churches and thronged the courts and all the near-by streets. Millions of small lights gleamed among the crowds, and the familiar sound of church bells filled the air continuously.

It was the night of a great holiday, and we birds shared in the gladness and the sense of gentle peace that brooded at that moment over human hearts.

It was a sweet greeting from our country—a welcome home!

On the third day we saw on the horizon the great Ostashkovo Marshes . . . our hummocks!

We were now flying, I believe, at a speed far greater

than that we had developed when we were trying to escape the memorable storm at sea.

We found our site in a far less attractive condition than that in which we left it. It was still very early in the spring. The snow had just melted away, and the first slender sprigs and grass blades piercing the fallow moss were visible here and there. But with every new day the landscape regained its former loveliness and, without wasting any time, we began to plan our encampment.

Our old nest was rightfully taken over by Papa and his new wife. Selecting the prettiest hummock, Blackneck and I built ours a few steps away. The Trifler and my sister were established a little farther off.

The work went on briskly and in a week everything was ready. What nests were those! Especially ours! I had the good luck to find a piece of old felt left in the fields by the shepherds. I tore it into pieces, and little by little carried it away. There was so much of it that, after our nest had been comfortably padded, there was still enough left for Papa and the Trifler.

Soon two delightful, greenish, brown-speckled eggs appeared in each of our nests. Under our safe protection, our companions began to brood over them in peace and quiet.

How quickly the required hatching period passed!

One day, when I came home with some food I saw in our nest two of the funniest-looking fledglings that were nevertheless very dear to my heart. I immediately shouted to my neighbor, the Trifler: "We have an increase in our family here!"

And his voice, already showing some signs of the hoarseness of maturity, sounded in reply: "Congratulations!"

THE END

235

CPSIA information can be obtained
at www.ICGtesting.com
Printed in the USA
BVHW091318290819
557143BV00017B/2504/P

9 781162 783697